Tutankhamun

Egypt's Most Famous Pharaoh

www.pocketessentials.com

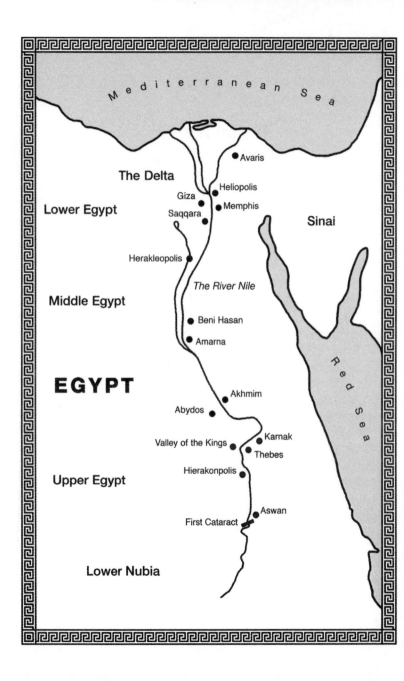

Tutankhamun

Egypt's Most Famous Pharaoh

BILL PRICE

POCKET ESSENTIALS

This edition published in 2007 by Pocket Essentials
P.O. Box 394, Harpenden, Herts, AL5 1XJ
www.pocketessentials.com
© Bill Price 2007
Editor: Nick Rennison
Index & Proofs: Richard Howard

A CIP catalogue record for this book is available from the British Library.

ISBN 978 1 84243 240 2
2 4 6 8 10 9 7 5 3 1

Typeset by Avocet Typeset, Chilton, Aylesbury, Bucks
Printed and bound in Great Britain by J.H. Haynes Ltd, Sparkford, Somerset

Contents

A Note on Dates

There is not one universally accepted chronology of Ancient Egypt, but the majority of them broadly agree with each other. Dates given for the reigns of particular rulers and for specific events are, on the other hand, much more widely disputed. These dates have been arrived at through different methods, the results of which rarely agree with each other, and are not necessarily as accurate or reliable as is sometimes made out. So, when reading anything about Ancient Egypt, the dates should always be taken as being approximate. For the sake of consistency, the dates given throughout this book follow the chronology set out in *The Oxford History of Ancient Egypt*, edited by Ian Shaw.

Introduction

Until the discovery of his tomb in 1922, Tutankhamun, the 12th Pharaoh of the 18th Dynasty, was one of the least known of all the pharaohs in the New Kingdom of Ancient Egypt. His immediate successors to the throne intentionally attempted to remove his name from history and, for more than 3,000 years, they were almost entirely successful. Ironically their actions would be one of the main reasons why the tomb was eventually found almost completely intact, while the tombs of those later pharaohs were robbed in antiquity. Shortly after his death Tutankhamun appears to have been forgotten and his tomb hidden under debris from the construction of another tomb, preserving it and its contents until it was uncovered by Howard Carter.

News of the discovery created a media sensation around the world, unprecedented in its scale for an archaeological find, and Tutankhamun was propelled out of obscurity and onto the front pages of the newspapers. The nature of the wonderful artefacts found in the tomb, many made of gold and inlaid with semi-precious stones, was a clear demonstration of the extraordinary wealth of the pharaohs of this period. One object in particular, the solid gold funeral mask, soon became the most recognised artefact from the ancient world and it is still considered by many to be the most beautiful.

Successive generations have been able to see some of these artefacts in touring exhibitions, including the latest one, 'Tutankhamun and the Pharaohs of the Golden Age'. The focus of this exhibition has been broadened from that of the previous ones to include objects associated with other pharaohs of the 18th Dynasty as well as Tutankhamun. This may have been done through necessity, as many of the best-known objects from the tomb, including the funeral mask, are no longer allowed to leave Egypt but it has resulted in Tutankhamun being placed in a greater historical context than in previous exhibitions.

Trends in archaeology in general have been towards gaining a wider knowledge of the ancient world, rather than simply appreciating the objects, so the new exhibition can be seen as following these developments. This approach is also the one followed in this book, which is primarily about Tutankhamun, but also attempts to place him in the context of the world in which he lived.

The details of the life of a young man who lived more than 3,000 years ago can never be known with absolute certainty, but archaeology is all about interpreting the available data to give as complete a picture as possible and, again, this is the approach followed here. Recent research and discoveries have also been incorporated, some of which tend to confirm interpretations made in the past while other findings conflict with some of the wilder speculation.

The line between interpretation and speculation can be a blurry one, particularly when dealing with a subject where concrete facts are hard to come by. In the following pages I have tried to stay on the right side of the line. Where more than one theory exists to explain a particular piece of evidence, I have presented the argument rather than chosen sides and, where conjecture has been employed, I have tried to make it plain that it is speculation and not fact.

Approaching Tutankhamun in this way, it becomes apparent that his reign coincided with one of the most fascinating and extraordinary periods in Egyptian history, the Amarna Period and its aftermath. It was also a time when Egypt was facing challenges from outside its borders, from the Hittites in the north and Nubia in the south, and from the vassal states within its own empire. By considering these events as well as the contents of the tomb, I hope that what emerges is a balanced account of the current state of our knowledge about Tutankhamun, together with an appreciation of those aspects of his life that are not yet fully understood.

Egypt and the Pharaohs

The Gift of the Nile

Herodotus famously described Egypt as being the gift of the Nile. The annual flood, beginning in July, deposited layers of silt over the inundated land along the banks of the river, building up a thick black alluvial soil. The Egyptians didn't need Herodotus to tell them about it. They called their country *Kennet*, 'the Black Land'. The Nile, rising as it does in the equatorial regions of Africa, flows all year round through the otherwise almost entirely arid region of Nubia and Egypt, on its 4,000-mile journey to the Mediterranean Sea. As well as laying down a rich and fertile soil, it was also a source of water for the irrigation of crops and the watering of animals and it provided a means of transport from one end of Egypt to the other. Boats could float down the Nile with the current and sail back up it on the prevailing southerly winds.

Agriculture was the foundation on which the wealth of Egypt developed. The first evidence of settled farming communities appears in the archaeological record much later than it does in the Fertile Crescent of what is now southern Turkey, Iraq, Syria and the Levant. In this area there is evidence of sedentism going back to the early Neolithic period, around 10,000 BC. During the same period, Egypt was sparsely populated with hunter-gatherers and, although they leave little evidence behind them, it is thought that nomadic pastoralists would also have passed through the area. The climate of North Africa as a whole was much wetter at that time and the Nile Valley was mostly made up of marshland, which was unsuitable for a settled way of life. By about 7000 BC, the climate in the region had dried out. Desert encroached over an enormous area that had previously been savannah, giving rise to the vast Sahara Desert. The marshes of the Nile Valley also dried out, leaving behind the thick soil of Egypt, perfect conditions for farming.

The first evidence of agriculture in Egypt comes from about 5000 BC around the Fayum Oasis to the west of the Nile. In the absence of any definite evidence, it is generally assumed that farming techniques spread into Egypt from the Levant, although it is difficult to say whether this was due to the movement of people or to the adoption of new technologies by people already living in the region. This is borne out by the type of agricultural practices found; crops included barley, emmer wheat (an early variety of wheat first domesticated in the Fertile Crescent) and flax and there is evidence of the presence of sheep, goats, cattle and pigs. Farming began in Upper Egypt at a later date, where the archaeological evidence suggests it spread from the south, from what is now Sudan, and from the Western Desert, rather than north along the Nile Valley.

Egyptian farmers may have made a slow start but, in such ideal conditions and once they began to make use of the annual flood and the irrigation potential of the Nile, the civilisation developed quickly. Within a thousand years the society that would go on to create the dynasties of Egypt had emerged. Small communities banded together to form king-doms and, either by agreement or conquest, a single united kingdom emerged to dominate the whole of Egypt.

The Dynasties of Egypt

In the third Century BC, about 200 years after Herodotus, the Greek-Egyptian priest Manetho wrote a history of Egypt going back to the beginning of the pharaonic period. Although his original work has not survived (in all likelihood, it was destroyed when the Library of Alexandria burnt down in 49 BC), it has been pieced together from extensive extracts quoted in works by later historians. In the *Aegptiaca*, as it was called, he set out a chronology of Ancient Egypt based on dividing the pharaohs into dynasties. Manetho almost certainly based his chronology on surviving pharaonic king lists, which were inscribed in stone and painted on the walls of tombs or, in some cases, written on papyrus. These formed part of the cult of the royal ancestors practised by the pharaohs. They could also have been used to legitimise the rule of a pharaoh by showing his relationship to previous pharaohs, thereby demonstrating his divine right to reign.

Although modifications have been made to Manetho's chronology many times, it remains the basis of the dating of Ancient Egypt still in use today. Deficiencies in the system have long been recognised and, as more information has come to light, it has become apparent that Egypt has not always consisted of a single unified society, ruled by one king who has then been succeeded by another in an orderly fashion. Dividing the dynasties into three kingdoms, the Old, Middle and New Kingdoms respectively, has partially overcome this problem. During the dynasties designated as belonging to one of these kingdoms, Egypt can be viewed as a single country comprising the Two Lands of Upper Egypt (the Nile Valley) and Lower Egypt (the Nile Delta). Between the kingdoms come the intermediate periods, during which the central power of a single king no longer existed and the region fractured into a number of smaller chiefdoms, each governed by its own local ruler. In a pattern repeated a number of times, one of these smaller powers grew in strength and overcame the others, reuniting Egypt and creating a single kingdom again.

Advances in archaeological dating techniques have allowed the chronologies to be refined further. Stratification, in which the descending layers of an archaeological dig are identified and the finds from the different layers compared with those from sites of known age, has been used for more than 100 years to give approximate datings. More recently techniques such as carbon dating, thermoluminescence and dendrochronology have further refined the chronology. As is the way of such things, the dates obtained by different methods don't always agree, leading to a certain amount of disagreement between dates in different accounts.

From Farmers to Pharaohs

Manetho gave the name of the first pharaoh as King Menes. No reference to this name has yet been found in the archaeological record and it has been suggested that Menes could be a mythological figure. Alternatively the name has been linked with Narmer, a predynastic ruler from about 3100 BC, or with Aha, the first pharaoh of the Early Dynasty Period, who ruled c3000 BC. What becomes apparent from the record is that the transition from an agricultural society based on individual settlements to a unified state governed by a single king was not a clear cut process and this means it is all but impossible to pinpoint the exact moment the pharaonic period in Egypt emerged.

The great Egyptologist Sir Flinders Petrie (1853-1942) considered that the complex society of Ancient Egypt could not have arisen from the indigenous peoples of the area and the society they inhabited prior to 3000 BC. Based on the evidence available at the beginning of the twentieth century, which suggested Egyptian society arose very rapidly, this was not an unreasonable conclusion to reach. Petrie thought complex society was introduced by the conquest of the lands of Egypt by a force from the south or, possibly, from the Levant and that the invasion resulted in the rise of a single ruler of all Egypt. More recent archaeological excavations have unquestionably shown that this was not the case and that the dynastic pharaohs were an indigenous phenomenon.

During the Naqata period, from 4000 BC to 3200 BC, the farming culture along the length of the Egyptian Nile began to become much more regular. Towards the end of this period the style of artefacts, such as pottery, found in archaeological excavations of sites throughout Egypt are much the same, suggesting the emergence of a single uniform culture at this time. This process began in Upper Egypt, where towns first began to develop out of scattered agricultural settlements and specialist trades began to be practised, and then spread down the Nile into Lower Egypt. The reason this occurred first in Upper Egypt is thought to have been that the greater availability of resources in this region allowed individual communities the opportunity to specialise in a particular trade or craft. The increasing wealth of particular towns, gained through trade links along the length of the Nile and south into Nubia, gave rise to a ruling elite. With increasing wealth came greater power and, as one local ruler became more powerful than his neighbouring rulers, the region began to become unified. There are two possible processes by which this can happen; it could have been a development of increasing trade links, with traders being followed by colonists, or it could have been accomplished by warfare and conquest. The most likely scenario is that Egypt was gradually united by a combination of both these processes, with those regions not submitting to the most powerful ruler voluntarily being overcome by force.

One of the main reasons why rulers from Upper Egypt wanted to extend their territory into Lower Egypt was so that they could gain complete control of the lucrative trade routes along the entire length of the Nile and further on across the Mediterranean into the Levant and Syria. One example, that of the timber trade between Egypt and what is now the Lebanon, serves to illustrate why this was the case. At that time the best wood to build large river-going boats and ships to sail the Mediterranean came from the cedars of Lebanon, tall straight-grained trees which do not grow in Egypt. The ruler of Upper Egypt had the natural resources and craft centres in towns to supply the wealth so that he could trade with the city states of the Lebanon, but he could only do so through the ports on the lower Nile and the Mediterranean coast of Egypt. There was an obvious advantage to be gained by developing direct links with the states in the Lebanon rather than having to go through any number of middle men in Lower Egypt or having to pay tariffs to local rulers for passage through their territory. Once one king became dominant in Upper Egypt, the prospect of his expanding his rule further, into Lower Egypt, must have been an attractive one.

Comparisons of the pottery of the period from various sites along the Nile reveal the replacement of the typical styles found in Lower Egypt with those deriving from the south. The obvious conclusion to draw from this is that the spreading culture of Upper Egypt came to dominate the whole region. It would make sense that not only pottery styles were becoming the same but the entire culture was becoming uniform under a single ruler.

Support for such a theory comes from excavations carried out at cemetery complexes in Abydos and Hieraknopolis, which both contain graves dating back to the early Naqata period. There is a gradual increase in both the quantity and quality of grave goods, indicating the rise of a complex hierarchical society. For example, the tomb designated as U-j in the Umm el-Qa'ab necropolis at Abydos, which dates to about 3150 BC, shows a clear line of development from earlier tombs in the same area, but it is much larger, extending to 12 rooms in all. Although it was robbed of much of its contents before it was excavated, numerous examples of pottery were found, including something like 400 wine jars from Palestine and 150 seals from other containers, which were inscribed with the earliest known examples of hieroglyphs. These, together with the presence of a wooden shrine and an ivory sceptre, point towards it being the tomb of a ruler, probably one of a number of pre-dynastic kings who share the name King Scorpion. There is not enough evidence to say for certain that this king definitely ruled both Upper and Lower Egypt, but the architectural style of the tomb is part of a progression which includes later kings who definitely did rule both lands. This shows that these later kings came originally from Upper Egypt.

As is the case with much of the archaeology of Egypt, the evidence is not specific enough to prove exactly when the unified state of Egypt arose but, by about 3000 BC, the structure of the state was in place. A state administration, using hieroglyphic writing to keep accounts, was based in Memphis, at the head of the Nile Delta, while the spiritual centre of Egypt remained in Upper Egypt, as it would throughout the entire course of the pharaonic history of the country. The prosperity of the country was based on agriculture and expanded its wealth through its natural resources and the high level of specialisation in particular crafts, such as metal working, and through trade and colonisation. It was held together by a strong state administration and by religious uniformity across the whole country, both under the direct control of a single ruler, who was held to be semi-divine by his subjects. This was the only country during this period in which a state of such size was ruled as a single entity by one king.

The Rise of the New Kingdom

The Old Kingdom lasted for about 800 years (see Appendix 1) and, during this period, many of the cultural, religious and political developments which would form the basis of future kingdoms first became established. Towards the end of the Old Kingdom, rival factions developed within the ruling elite, resulting in the First Intermediate Period, when Egypt splintered into several smaller states. After the reunification of the Two Lands during the Middle Kingdom, which lasted from about 2055 BC to 1650 BC, a similar process appears to have occurred, splitting the country up again during the 13th Dynasty and leading to the Second Intermediate Period. Like the First Intermediate Period, this was a time when there was not a single ruler of a unified country. The political situation was complex and constantly changing, with shifting alliances forming and breaking between the rulers of different regions and power struggles and open warfare erupting between rival factions.

The Turin Royal Canon, a fragmentary king list written in the thirteenth century BC, during the reign of Ramesses II, and now held in the Egyptian Museum in Turin, names more than 100 kings from the Second Intermediate Period, which lasted for little more than 100 years. This gives a good indication of the volatile nature of the times, where different kings ruled regions of what had previously been a single country for relatively short spans of time, before being dethroned by other more powerful rulers.

During the Middle Kingdom Egypt had expanded south, beyond the First Cataract of the Nile at what is now Aswan, the traditional boundary of the country, and into Nubia. The primary reason for this conquest was to annex the huge mineral resources to be found in Wawat, the region of Lower Nubia between the Nile and the Red Sea which was particularly rich in gold. The extraordinary wealth of the Egyptian state was based on these goldmines but, as the country fragmented during the Second Intermediate Period, the Kushite Kingdom of Nubia seized the opportunity to regain control of Wawat. As well as being threatened by Kush from the south,

Egypt was being undermined from within by the Hyksos, who gained control of most of Lower Egypt, up to and including Memphis, thus reducing the area ruled by Egyptian kings to Upper Egypt alone.

The identity of the Hyksos is a mystery. They left no written records behind them, so they are only known from highly biased Egyptian accounts of the period and from what can be gathered from the archaeological remains. The Egyptian term 'Hyksos' literally means 'kings from foreign lands'. Although it is generally used now to refer to all of the people who gained control of Lower Egypt during the Second Intermediate Period, the Egyptians called the general population 'the aanu', often translated as 'Asiatics' because the Hyksos appear to have come into Egypt from Palestine and Syria. This theory is supported by the names given to the Hyksos kings in the Turin Canon, which derive from the Semitic languages of South West Asia. It is thought that they began to arrive in Egypt from about 1800 BC and may originally have been what we would now call economic migrants, moving to the country to find work. Their numbers were increased by the arrival of prisoners of war, taken in the military campaigns mounted by Egypt in Palestine during the Middle Kingdom, and brought back to Egypt as slaves. Evidence of warfare on Egypt's eastern border, in the form of defensive fortifications, suggests prolonged periods of conflict with Palestine at this time, although there is no evidence of the Hyksos arriving in Egypt as the result of conquest.

The Hyksos established a capital at Avaris, in the Nile Delta, and gradually extended their territory, pushing the indigenous Egyptian rulers further south. They gained control of Memphis, the Egyptian capital at the head of the delta, from where they could control the boat traffic on the Nile. The Egyptians considered themselves to be the natural rulers of their country and inscriptions concerning the Hyksos which date from this period either complain about having to have the permission of these foreign intruders to travel along the Nile or make grand claims about defeating them in battle. Although the chronology from this period is not entirely clear, the Egyptian rulers of Upper Egypt who make up the 17th Dynasty were constantly attempting to regain the territory they had lost to the Hyksos and were also involved in fighting in Nubia.

Two stelae erected in the Temple of Amun in Karnak, the religious complex near Thebes (and the modern city of Luxor), by Kamose, the last king of the 17th Dynasty who ruled from 1555 to 1550 BC, give details of the campaigns he conducted against the Hyksos. These campaigns began under the previous pharaoh Seqenenra Taa and they were continued by Ahmose, who reigned from 1550 to 1525 BC. Wall reliefs carved during his reign at Abydos in Upper Egypt show the king at the head of a battle fleet on the Nile, which, together with an Egyptian army equipped with horses and chariots, is attacking Avaris. The city was besieged for a period of several years before a treaty was agreed between Ahmose and the Hyksos king which resulted in the Hyksos giving up the city. They retreated into Palestine, a movement of a large number of people which has sometimes been interpreted as the source of the biblical story of the Exodus, when Moses led the Israelites out of Egypt. However, this interpretation has been disputed and there are numerous other theories which attempt to identify the events of the Exodus with events at different times in Egyptian history.

Ahmose was eventually successful in his campaigns against the Hyksos and, at some point towards the end of his 25-year reign, the Two Lands of Egypt were reunited. An inscription found in the tomb of one of his military leaders describes Ahmose continuing the campaign into Palestine and, after a three-year siege, sacking the city of Sharuhen, near Gaza. As a result of his success in these campaigns, reuniting Egypt under the rule of the Theban pharaohs, Ahmose, although he was the son of a pharaoh of the 17th Dynasty, is considered to be the first king of the 18th Dynasty, and responsible for establishing the New Kingdom.

The Golden Age

The military campaigns of Kamose and Ahmose were consolidated and built upon by Ahmose's son and successor as pharaoh, Amenhotep I, who ruled from 1525 BC to 1504 BC. He extended the empire in the south, gaining control of Upper Nubia, including the region of Wawat and the Nubian goldmines. With the Theban pharaohs in control of the trade routes and the goldmines, Egypt entered a period of great prosperity, sometimes known as the Golden Age of the Pharaohs, which would last for the next 500 years.

Both Ahmose and Amenhotep I began an extensive programme of monumental building work at the important religious sites across the country, particularly Memphis and Karnak, and also at Avaris, the former Hyksos capital on the eastern edge of the delta. The links established between Egypt and the Mediterranean can be seen from the wall decorations of one of these buildings in Avaris, which is in the Minoan style. At this time Crete and the islands of the Aegean were some of the most important mercantile centres in the region, thought to be particularly involved in the trade in tin and copper, the constituents of bronze. Another indicator of the changing fortunes of the Theban pharaohs can be seen from the increasing size and complexity of the tombs being built during this period, together with the extensive use of precious metals, particularly gold, in their grave goods.

During the reign of Amenhotep I most of the characteristics of society and culture found throughout the rest of the 18th Dynasty were established. Amenhotep, which means 'Amun is satisfied', identified himself particularly with the sun god Amun, the local god of Thebes, and the Temple of Amun at Karnak. He continued the territorial gains made in Nubia, guaranteeing the continued wealth of the country, during the 21 years of his reign, but appears to have died without a surviving heir. He was succeeded by Thutmose I, a high-ranking member of the Theban court, who is thought to have been related to Amenhotep I by marriage to the pharaoh's daughter.

Although the royal women of the 18th Dynasty, with the odd notable exception, rarely became pharaohs themselves, they played an important part in the succession of kingship from one pharaoh to the next. Marriage to the pharaoh's daughter was an important part of conferring legitimacy on the claims to the throne of an heir, even if he was the pharaoh's son, and is one reason why many pharaohs of the 18th Dynasty married female members of their own family. Another reason for this was that, while it was acceptable for a male member of the royal family to marry a commoner, it was not considered fitting for a royal woman to do so. According to court etiquette a princess could only marry someone of an equivalent or higher rank.

The lineage established by Thutmose I lasted for the next 175 years, until it was extinguished by the death of Tutankhamun, his last direct descendant. Thutmose II succeeded his father, but died after reigning for only three years. His son, Thutmose III, was very young at this time, perhaps only three or four years old, and succeeded to the throne, with his aunt Hatshepsut acting as regent. Although not Thutmose III's mother, Hatshepsut was the Great Royal Wife of Thutmose II.

The royal women held considerable power and important positions in the religious life of the country throughout the 18th Dynasty. The mothers, wives and daughters of the pharaoh became much more prominent than women had been in any of the preceding periods. This prominence began with Ahmose-Nefertari, the wife of Amenhotep I, and continued with Hatshepsut, who ruled in the style of a male pharaoh for the first 20 years of Thutmose III's reign.

After the first few years of Hatshepsut's regency, she declared herself to be the legitimate ruler and, over the next 20 years, she reigned as pharaoh, with Thutmose III remaining in the background. It was a peaceful and prosperous time for the country, allowing Hatshepsut to engage in an extensive monumental building programme, including a mortuary temple at Deir el-Bahri on the west bank of the Nile, near the entrance to the Valley of the Kings and now one of the most visited sites in Upper Egypt. In a wall painting found in the temple Hatshepsut is shown leading a trading mission to the Land of Punt, on the Red Sea coast, and there are also a number of inscriptions which appear to be an attempt to give legitimacy to her reign. She is shown wearing the sacred false beard of the pharaoh, a sign of the divine nature of the position, and her name is spelt as if she were a man.

After Hatshepsut's death, she was buried in a tomb in the Valley of the Kings, possibly in the same tomb as her father Thutmose I, the one designated as KV20 in the modern numbering system of the tombs in the valley. At a later date, she was moved to another tomb, KV60. Dr Zahi Hawass, Secretary General of the Egyptian Supreme Council of Antiquities and one of the most prominent modern Egyptologists, announced in June 2007 that a mummy recovered from tomb KV60 by Howard Carter in 1903, which had been lost in the Egyptian Museum in Cairo for many years, had been found and identified as that of Hatshepsut. DNA analysis was used to establish the relationship between the mummy and Ahmose-Nefertari and the identification was confirmed, at least to the satisfaction of Dr Hawass, by a CT scan, which was used to compare a tooth found in a canopic jar bearing Hatshepsut's name in a mummy cache from Deir el-Barhi (designated DB320), with a gap in the KV60 mummy's teeth. The scan showed the tooth was a perfect match for the gap and also revealed that Hatshepsut suffered from osteoporosis and severe arthritis and died at the age of about 50 from liver and bone cancer.

Thutmose III became pharaoh on his own after Hatshepsut's death in about 1458 BC and reigned for a further 30 years. He conducted numerous successful military campaigns in Syria-Palestine and in Nubia, known because they were recorded by the royal scribe Thanuny, and these gave him a reputation as one of the greatest of all the warrior-pharaohs. The Egyptian Empire reached its greatest extent at this time, stretching from the north Syrian kingdom of Niya to the Fourth Cataract of the Nile in Nubia. Although the accounts may not be totally reliable, Thanuny also records the Babylonians and Assyrians, two kingdoms from beyond the Euphrates river in modern Iraq, paying tribute to Thutmose III, as well as the Hittites from further north in Anatolia. He does not mention the Mitanni, the other major power in the region, presumably because they had not submitted to the pharaoh.

Towards the end of Thutmose III's reign attempts were made to remove all references to Hatshepsut from the inscriptions on monuments built during her rule. It is not entirely clear why Thutmose would wait more than 20 years to begin this process if it was motivated by revenge on Hatshepsut, who had ruled in his place. An alternative explanation for the attempted destruction of Hatshepsut's name was that Thutmose, towards the end of his life, was attempting to ensure the succession of his son, the future Amenhotep II, at the expense of rival claims to the throne by other relatives of Hatshepsut.

For the first two years of his reign Amenhotep III shared the throne with his father as the coregent, perhaps another method of ensuring the succession. After the death of Thutmose III in about 1425 BC, Amenhotep II continued to maintain the territorial gains made by his father in Syria and Nubia. He also appears to have reached some form of accommodation with the Mitanni, perhaps by the exchange of princesses between the two royal households, as hostility between the two empires ceased during his reign. It ushered in a period of peace and this, together with the flow of wealth into Egypt from the northern and southern ends of its empire, led to a period of great prosperity which would continue for more than 50 years.

Thutmose IV succeeded Amenhotep II and ruled for about ten years, from 1400 BC to 1390 BC. He is perhaps best known for the Dream Stele, a stone slab erected between the front paws of the Great Sphinx of Giza and inscribed with a text which carries a justification for his rise to the throne instead of his older brother. It describes a dream he claims to have had while resting under the head of the sphinx, which was buried up to its neck in sand at that time. In the dream the sphinx tells Thutmose that, if he clears all sand away from around it and restores its body, he will become the next pharaoh.

Like all the other pharaohs of the 18th Dynasty, Thutmose IV initiated large-scale building projects as soon as he came to power, particularly at the Temple of Amun in Karnak, where, among many other buildings, he was responsible for the tallest obelisk ever erected in Egypt. After being removed from Egypt in AD 3, during the reign of the Roman Emperor Caligula, this now stands in St. Peter's Square in the Vatican.

Since his Great Royal Wife Nefertari does not appear to have had any surviving male children, Thutmose IV was succeeded on his death by Amenhotep III, his son with Mutemwiya, one of his minor wives, Amenhotep III became the ninth pharaoh of the 18th Dynasty and his reign of about 38 years, from 1390 BC to 1352 BC, would be looked back on as a time of peace and prosperity to which future generations wished to return. His Great Royal Wife Tiye, who would survive him by a number of years, was not of the royal blood line. She was the daughter of the prominent courtiers Yuya and Tuyu, sometimes also said to be the parents of Ay, who would succeed Tutankhamun as pharaoh. Amenhotep III and Tiye had at least two sons, the oldest of whom, another

Thutmose, died before his father, leaving the second son to succeed to the throne as Amenhotep IV. He would later change his name to Akhenaten. It would be during his rule, from 1352 BC to 1336 BC, that the great empire established by his ancestors would begin to unravel.

Akhenaten's tumultuous reign and the Amarna Period are dealt with more fully in the following two chapters, as he is the person generally acknowledged as most likely to have been Tutankhamun's father. One of the consequences of his rule was a concerted attempt by later pharaohs to destroy everything he had built and obliterate all reference to him from any inscriptions. The campaign to wipe him out of history was a successful one, so much so that it is now diffi-cult to reconstruct the events of his reign, particularly the later part and the succession of Tutankhamun. Akhenaten's Great Royal Wife Nefertiti, who has become famous in modern times through the beautiful bust of her now in the Altes Museum in Berlin, extended the already considerable powers she held and is thought to have ruled as an equal with Akhenaten during the later part of the Amarna Period.

Akhenaten ruled for about 17 years and Nefertiti's name disappears from the record after about the 14th year. A number of theories, none of which can be fully supported with the evidence as it currently stands, have been put forward to explain what happened at this time. One possi-bility is that Nefertiti changed her name to the male name Neferneferuaten and ruled as co-regent with Akhenaten, becoming pharaoh herself for a few years after his death. An alternative theory says she died during Akhenaten's 14th regnal year, possibly as the result of an outbreak of an epidemic which swept through Egypt at this time, and that

Akhenaten was succeeded by Smenkhare, who was either his younger brother or oldest son. Yet another theory has Meritaten, Nefertiti's daughter, taking on the role of pharaoh herself or becoming Smenkhare's Great Royal Wife in order to give his reign the required legitimacy.

The only thing that can be said for certain is that our knowledge of what happened at the end of Akhenaten's reign and of how Tutankhamun succeeded to the throne is currently not sufficient to be able to untangle the actual events. It will take some major new discoveries in Egypt to make the situation clear. In the meantime, it can at least be said with some degree of conviction that Tutankhamun ascended to the throne within a few years of Akhenaten's death.

The Life of Tutankhamun

The Unknown Pharaoh

Up until the discovery of Tutankhamun's tomb in 1922, he was one of the least-known of the 18th Dynasty pharaohs. His name appeared on some king lists and was mentioned by Manetho, who gave his name as Rathotis, but that was about all that remained. The extraordinary artefacts found in the tomb added greatly to our knowledge of him and of the 18th Dynasty in general, but, as ungrateful as it might sound, there were some disappointing aspects to the discovery. Howard Carter himself acknowledged this. The tomb was quite poorly decorated when compared with the tombs of many of the other pharaohs interred in the Valley of the Kings. Only the burial chamber itself had plastered and painted walls, and it contained no inscriptions or papyri giving details of Tutankhamun's life, as Carter expected and hoped to find.

A great deal can be learned about Tutankhamun and Egyptian life during the 18th Dynasty in general from a detailed analysis of the contents of the tomb, but the information thus gained does not lead to any solid biographical details. Carter compared what can be gathered about Tutankhamun from his tomb to attempting to write a biography of someone by visiting the place where he lived without having access to diaries, letters or anything else he may have written. It is possible to construct an overall picture, but not to get to know the real person or what he actually did during his life.

The tomb was the only one of a pharaoh ever found in the Valley of the Kings that had not been comprehensively robbed long before the discovery, but many of the other pharaohs left behind numerous monuments containing inscriptions about events occurring during their lifetimes. Almost every reference to Tutankhamun was removed from the record and, after he died, his name was chiselled out of any inscriptions written during his lifetime, so this avenue of investigation into his life is also severely limited. It is not particularly unusual for this to happen but, in Tutankhamun's case, the removal of his name was particularly comprehensive and successful. The reason he was treated in this way after his death is related to his associations with Akhenaten, the heretic pharaoh, and to the fact that he died without an heir, resulting in attempts by later pharaohs to disguise the information that they were not related to a pharaoh who had gone before them, information which might have invalidated their claims to the throne.

The success of the campaign to remove Tutankhamun's name from history is the main reason why we now know so little about him but, because he appears to have been completely forgotten not long after his death, it also resulted in the location of his tomb in the Valley of the Kings being forgotten. The tomb was entered by robbers on more than one occasion shortly after it was first sealed but they appear to have been disturbed by the necropolis guards, a police force employed by the pharaohs in an attempt to prevent robberies, before doing very much damage. The entrance to the tomb, which is low down in the Valley of the Kings, became filled in with the debris from the construction of another tomb and was forgotten, probably the only reason it escaped the attentions of later tomb robbers.

The rest of this chapter concerns what is actually known about the life of Tutankhamun. With so few concrete facts to go on, it is tempting to write what would be a fictional biography of Tutankhamun, based on the huge amount of speculation surrounding his life, but, rather than that, what follows is a discussion of the available evidence, such as it is, together with reasonable and sensible interpretations of that evidence.

What's in a Name?

The pharaohs of the New Kingdom idolised their predecessors from the Middle Kingdom. It was one of the main motivating factors for the reunification of the Two Lands at the start of the 18th Dynasty, which represented what the pharaohs considered to be the restoration of their rightful position. Many of the old practices followed by the pharaohs of the Middle Kingdom were begun again, including the use of their naming system for the ruler. The standardised form, written out in full on inscriptions in tombs and stelae, shows each pharaoh adopting a name consisting of five parts, known as the royal titulary or, sometimes, the fivefold titulary. Some of these names were ceremonial titles, only used on formal occasions, and they can be compared to the names and titles used by the current British Royal Family. Some of Prince Charles's titles, for example, are His Royal Highness the Prince of Wales, the Earl of Chester, the Duke of Cornwall and the Lord of the Isles. Most of these titles are not generally used, except on particular state occasions, and he is usually known as Prince Charles or the Prince of Wales, rather like a pharaoh would usually be known by his nomen and praenomen.

Tutankhamun is the universally accepted form of the pharaoh's name used in modern times, although, since the exact Egyptian pronunciation is not known, the spelling can sometimes vary. This is actually his personal name, or nomen, which was the name given to a royal prince at birth. In Tutankhamun's case, he was originally named Tutankhaten, which translates to 'the Living Image of Aten', but, for religious reasons, he changed his nomen to Tutankhamun, 'the Living Image of Amun', soon after becoming pharaoh. The reasons for the change are expanded on in Chapter 3, but essentially it occurred at the same time as the reformation of the old religious order under Tutankhamun, and a return to the worship of a pantheon of Egyptian gods, chief amongst which was Amun, after the rise of the single god Aten under Akhenaten. At the time of his succession to the throne, the full nomen adopted was Tutankhamun Hekaiunushema, 'the Living Image of Amun, Ruler of Heliopolis', a deliberate reference to the sun god as worshipped by the Priesthood of Amun at Karnak.

The nomen, when written, was usually prefaced by the term 'son of Ra', one of the principal gods worshipped throughout Egyptian history. It was surrounded by a cartouche, an elliptical outline thought to symbolise the protection of the pharaoh, or, possibly, to be a diagram of the sun circling the universe. The only other name similarly enclosed was the throne name, or praenomen, which, in Tutankhamun's case, was Nebkhepepure, 'Lord of the Forms of Ra'. This was usually accompanied by the title Nesu-bity, translated variously as 'the King of the Upper and Lower Lands' or 'He of the Sedge and Bee', where the sedge symbolizes Upper Egypt and the bee Lower Egypt. The duality of the name can also be seen as a reference to the pharaoh's position as both a mortal man and the earthly manifestation of a god.

These two names, the nomen and praenomen, were those usually used in Egypt to refer to Tutankhamun and are primarily concerned with his position as the king of the Two Lands, the ruler of earthly matters. The other three names stress the pharaoh's role as the manifestation of the divine, his place in the spiritual realm rather than the earthly one. The first of these is the Horus name. It is the oldest of the names used in the royal titulary, emerging in the pre-dynastic period, where it was used to identify the pharaoh with the falcon god Horus. By the time of the New Kingdom, pharaohs were more likely to be identified with Ra, but the form of the name remained the same. Tutankhamun's Horus name was Kanakht Tutmesut, 'the Strong Bull, Pleasing at Birth'. The fourth name, the Nebty name, was associated with the vulture and cobra goddesses Nekhbet and Wadjyt and can be translated as 'One of Perfect Form, Who Purifies the Two Lands' and 'Great of the Palace of Amun and Lord of All'. The Golden Horus name, thought to convey Tutankhamun's eternal name for the afterlife, changed throughout his lifetime. One version can be translated as 'He who wears the crown and pleases the gods, Ruler of Truth who pleases the gods, who wears the crown of his father Ra and who wears the crown uniting the Two Lands'.

Where the royal titulary was written out in full, the names were placed in a conventional order, starting with the three divine names and followed by the praenomen, with the nomen, Tutankhamun, placed last.

The Question of Parentage

Very little can be said with absolute certainty about Tutankhamun's parentage. There are only two references to him in this context still in existence, an indication of the thoroughness with which later pharaohs attempted to remove his name from the record. One of these is an inscription on a block of stone found on the west bank of the Nile at Ashmunew, which is directly across the river from Amarna, from where it is thought to have originated. It describes Tutankhamun as the son of a king, saying 'the king's bodily son, his beloved Tutankhaten'. Unfortunately the inscription does not contain the name of the king to whom it refers but, at least, it is possible to say from this that Tutankhamun was more than likely of royal blood, a statement Howard Carter felt unable to make based on the contents of the tomb.

The other known inscription is contained in a frieze decorating the wall of the processional colonnade in the Temple of Luxor, originally built by Amenhotep III and continued by Tutankhamun. It depicts the Festival of Opet, an important yearly ritual which re-enacted a pharaoh's coronation, thereby confirming his rule, and it is one of the very few surviving temple reliefs from the reign of Tutankhamun, perhaps one missed by those who attempted to obliterate all references to him. In the inscription, Tutankhamun describes Amenhotep III as his father which, if correct, would make him Akhenaten's brother. There is some disagreement about the correct translation and usage of the hieroglyph used for the term 'father'. It has been suggested by some scholars that it refers to Amenhotep III as a direct ancestor of Tutankhamun, rather than as his actual father. An examination of the dates known for the two pharaohs would tend to confirm this latter interpretation. Tutankhamun was born in about 1344 BC and Akhenaten succeeded Amenhotep III in 1352 BC, which means Tutankhamun was born eight years after Akhenaten came to the throne. Unless Amenhotep III lived for a long period after Akhenaten gained the throne, or they ruled together as co-regents for at least those eight years, Tutankhamun could not have been Amenhotep III's son. There are precedents for a co-regency between a father and son in Egypt but the ones that are known only lasted a much shorter period, usually a year or two at the most. It appears highly unlikely that, if a co-regency between Amenhotep III and Akhenaten existed at all, it could have lasted for the required amount of time.

If the above argument is accepted, then the most likely candidate for Tutankhamun's father becomes Akhenaten himself. The eighth year of Akhenaten's reign came right in the middle of the Amarna period so, assuming the inscription found at Ashmunew saying that Tutankhamun was the son of a king is correct, then Akhenaten is the only really viable candidate. A theory suggesting that Smenkhare, the mysterious figure who was possibly Tutankhamun's immediate predecessor, was his father can not be dismissed completely but, with virtually no evidence to go on at all, it can not be confirmed either. Smenkhare was certainly not the pharaoh at the time of Tutankhamun's birth and, if he was any relation at all, he is more likely to have been Tutankhamun's uncle or older brother.

Needless to say, the identity of Tutankhamun's mother is no less problematic. If he was indeed Akhenaten's son, the first candidate to be his mother is Nefertiti, who bore the title of Great Royal Wife. The problem with this is that Nefertiti is only known to have given birth to six daughters and there is no evidence of her having any sons. Wall paintings and reliefs in Akhenaten's tomb in Amarna clearly show the couple with their daughters, but never with any male children. This does not mean that Nefertiti definitely did not have any sons, as it was conventional during the 18th Dynasty for there to be no depictions of any of a pharaoh's male children. Showing a male heir could be interpreted as compromising the position of the pharaoh, presenting him as a mortal rather than as a god. It might also pose questions about the line of succession which were too sensitive to be aired in such a public way. Daughters, on the other hand, presented no threat and represented continuity in the royal household so they were regularly shown. Nefertiti, then, can not be ruled out as a candidate to be Tutankhamun's mother.

Another relief found in Akhenaten's tomb is thought to show one of his other wives, known as Kiya. Speculation that she was a Mitanni princess who was sent to Akhenaten's court to maintain friendly relations between the two countries remains entirely unproven, but there is no doubt she held a privileged position in the royal household. The titles she held included 'Greatly Beloved Wife' and 'the Favourite' which, it has been suggested, could have been granted to her because she gave birth to a male heir to the throne. The relief in the tomb shows a woman lying in a bed, with a figure standing next to her holding a child of indeterminate sex. One interpretation of this scene is that it shows Kiya on her deathbed with the future pharaoh Tutankhamun being held by a wet nurse but, unfortunately, the depiction is not clear enough to be able to say this for certain.

In the absence of any conclusive evidence, the majority of the literature on Tutankhamun has settled on Akhenaten and Kiya as being the most likely of the candidates to be his parents. To date the Egyptian authorities have not allowed DNA analysis to be carried out on Tutankhamun's mummy but, should this situation change, this would be the most likely avenue of further research into his parentage. Even with this, though, there is a problem. The mummies of Akhenaten, Kiya or any of the other likely candidates have not been found, or, at least, have not been identified, so, even if a DNA test was carried out on Tutankhamun, there is nothing with which to compare his DNA.

Marriage and Children

Nothing can be said with any degree of conviction about Tutankhamun's early years. Presumably he grew up in the privileged position of a prince in the royal household of Akhenaten in Amarna. After Akhenaten's death and the confusion surrounding the succession, which involved Smenkhare and possibly Nefertiti, Tutankhamun became pharaoh at the age of about eight or nine. Very shortly before gaining the throne, or possibly very shortly afterwards, he married Ankhesenpaaten, probably his half-sister, who, in line with her husband, changed her name to Ankhesenamun, which means 'She Who Lives Through Amun'. She was the third daughter of Akhenaten and Nefertiti and was about five or six years older than Tutankhamun.

There is nothing to suggest there was any doubt about Tutankhamun's right to succeed Akhenaten (how could anyone other than a prince gain the throne at the age of nine?) but marrying a senior royal princess would have completely legitimised his claim. It would also have been unthinkable under the strict conventions of the pharaoh's household for a commoner to marry a senior princess of the royal blood line. Marriage between such close relatives was a common feature because it was considered that princesses should only marry those of a suitable status, which often limited their options to other members of their family. Ankhesenamun herself had been married to her father before she was married to Tutankhamun, making her his step-mother as well as his half-sister and wife, and she may also have been married to Smenkhare as well. It is possible that Ankhesenamun had a daughter from the marriage to her father, a child called Ankhesenpaaten Tasherit (Tasherit means the younger or little one), but the parentage of this girl is not known for sure. If Ankhesenamun was the mother, she must have been very young when her daughter was born. Ankhesenpaaten Tasherit appears to have been born in the last year of Akhenaten's life, when Ankhesenamun would have been about twelve or thirteen.

The marriage between Tutankhamun and Ankhesenamun may have been a political one, intended to prove to the people of Egypt that Tutankhamun was the rightful heir to the throne, but images of the couple found in Tutankhamun's tomb suggest a close bond between the two of them. One of the best-known of these is on the back panel of a chair from the antechamber of the tomb known as the Golden Throne. It is very much in the informal style of the Amarna Period and this, together with the fact that the inscribed names have been changed from the original 'Aten' versions to the 'Amun' ones, suggests that it dates to an early period of their marriage. The figures are formed out of silver, coloured glass and faience (a type of glazed earthenware) inlaid into sheets of gold. The royal husband and wife are in a floral pavilion, which is open at the top to allow the rays of the Aten, the sun disc, through. Ankhesenamun is standing in front of the seated figure of Tutankhamun and has a vessel in one hand. She is reaching out to Tutankhamun with the other hand as if she is about to rub ointment or perfume into his shoulder. This depiction of the royal couple is unusual in its intimacy, even by the relaxed standards of the Amarna Period, and shows what can only be described as a close attachment between two people.

Another discovery in the tomb was described by Howard Carter as the saddest thing he had ever found. Two small anthropoid (human-shaped) coffins had been placed together in a plain wooden box, which was piled up with a number of other boxes and an assortment of artefacts in the treasury of the tomb. They contained the mummified bodies of two little girls. One had been miscarried after about five months of pregnancy and is thought to have been stillborn. The other was either stillborn at about eight or nine months or died during childbirth. X-rays of this mummy showed that the little girl suffered from a number of congenital disorders, including spina bifida, making it unlikely she would have survived very long had she been born alive. Although there were no indications of who these two children were, it can only be presumed that they were the daughters of Tutankhamun and Ankhesenamun. There is no evidence that the couple had any other children so, when Tutankhamun died, he left no heirs.

The Boy King

It was not unprecedented for a pharaoh to ascend to the throne at such a young age during the 18th Dynasty. Thutmose III and Amenhotep III were both very young when they became pharaoh but, in both cases, the Great Royal Wife of their father acted as regent until they were old enough to take on the full responsibility of being pharaoh themselves. This was not an option for Tutankhamun as he appears to have had no surviving older relatives other than his wife. The role of regent was undertaken by the commander-in-chief of the army, Horemheb, who held great power in Tutankhamun's court, together with the senior adviser Ay, who had previously held high positions with both Amenhotep III and Akhenaten.

At some stage during the first or second year of Tutankhamun's reign, he abandoned the city established by Akhenaten at Amarna, returning the political and administrative capital to Memphis and restoring Thebes as the religious centre of the country. In a later inscription, some years after Tutankhamun's death, Horemheb took credit for this decision, suggesting that the military might have played a major role in restoring the old religion of the country. It is, of course, also possible that Horemheb was writing the history of the period in order to cast himself in the most favourable light.

Prior to Akhenaten, who appears to have spent the majority of his time in his capital in Amarna, the pharaoh travelled extensively throughout the Two Lands, staying in royal palaces in different cities as they did so. As well as exerting the authority of the king by being seen frequently by his subjects, the pharaoh, as the semi-divine religious leader of the country, presided over many religious festivals occurring at different times of the year in different parts of the country. Presumably Tutankhamun, having abandoned the new religious system imposed on the country by Akhenaten, would have returned to these royal duties himself. When not travelling he would have probably spent the majority of his time in his main palaces in Memphis and Thebes and at the smaller palace constructed for him not far from the Great Sphinx of Giza. This appears to have had been a hunting lodge and was situated in the region traditionally used by the Egyptian royal family for that purpose. Judging by the number of times hunting is represented in the decorations of the tombs of many different pharaohs, it was a favourite pastime enjoyed over many generations by the royal family. Perhaps it was also where royal princes developed such skills as driving a chariot and shooting a bow which they would be expected to have to become military leaders.

The range of weaponry and hunting equipment found in Tutankhamun's tomb gives a clear indication of these pastimes. About thirty bows of various sizes and designs, including sophisticated compound bows, and more than a hundred arrows had been placed in the tomb for Tutankhamun to take with him into the afterlife, perhaps indicating the favourite hunting method of the pharaoh. There are also a number of illustrations of hunting scenes, including, in one example, the gilded decoration on the disc-shaped handle of an ostrich feather fan. Tutankhamun is shown taking aim at an ostrich with his bow and arrow from his chariot, drawn by two magnificently adorned horses at full gallop. A dog runs alongside the horses, snapping at the heels of the ostrich, which has already been hit by an arrow, and another ostrich lies on the ground in front of it. An inscription commemorates what it describes as the events of an actual hunt in which Tutankhamun killed two ostriches. The feathers from these ostriches, the inscription goes on to say, were the ones used to make the fan itself.

A similar scene was painted on the lid of a beautifully decorated chest found in the antechamber of the tomb and known as the Painted Box, except Tutankhamun is shown this time hunting antelopes and he is followed by a large retinue. On the side of the box, he is shown in a similar pose, drawing his bow from the back of a chariot, but this time he is aiming at the massed ranks of a Syrian army and is being followed into battle by other chariots of the Egyptian army. It is one of a number of depictions of Tutankhamun engaged in military action. In a scene on a ceremonial shield, he is shown as a sphinx trampling over the prostrate bodies of his Nubian enemies. Here he is being represented as the victorious, semi-divine ruler of the Two Lands who is protecting his people from hostile countries at the borders of the empire.

There were plenty of items of military equipment in the tomb, including swords, daggers and shields, most of which were highly decorated and gilded, and clearly intended for ceremonial purposes. Some, however, were more practical in nature and showed signs of having been used. Whether this can be taken as a confirmation that Tutankhamun himself took part in military campaigns, as many of the pharaohs before him in the 18th Dynasty certainly did, is open to question. The depictions could be just symbolic representations of Tutankhamun as the protector of his people, while the actual job of fighting Egypt's enemies was carried out by the army, led by Horemheb.

Other objects found in the tomb show the pharaoh as the political leader of the country. There are a number of representations of Tutankhamun wearing various ceremonial regalia associated with his position as king of the Two Lands and the rest of the Egyptian Empire. Figurines variously show him wearing different crowns; the rounded and pointed white crown of Upper Egypt and the flatter red crown of the delta. In some pictures he is seen wearing a combination of the two, together with the stripped nemes head-cloth. In typical representations, the pharaoh is shown holding a shepherd's crook and flail, often, but not always, with his hands crossed over his chest. These can be taken as symbolic of the agricultural base of Egypt and of the pharaoh looking after his people as a farmer looks after his animals and crops, but, as with many Egyptian representations, they also have a number of other complex meanings and associations. The flail, for example, was associated with Osiris, the god of both fertility and death and, perhaps, as a combination of the two, resurrection, and the crook was also a symbol of the pharaoh as head of the government.

As well as Horemheb and Ay, the names of some other officials in Tutankhamun's administration are known, mostly through inscriptions in their own tombs in the Saqqara necropolis near Memphis. The chief of the treasury was a man called Maya, who was responsible for collecting and distributing the tax revenue of the country. This would have involved paying for the building work carried out by Tutankhamun to erect temples and palaces, particularly at Karnak, and to reverse the work done by Akhenaten. Maya is also thought to have been in control of the royal necropolis, where he would have supervised the transfer of the royal mummies, including

Akhenaten, from their original burial places in Amarna to tombs in the Valley of the Kings. Later he also appears to have played an important part in the burials of Tutankhamun, Ay and Horemheb.

Not very much is known about Usermont and Pentu other than that they held the important positions of viziers of Upper and Lower Egypt. Vizier is the term used by Egyptologists to describe the position of chief minister or governor of one of the Two Lands. The holders of these positions would have been the most powerful men in Egypt after the pharaoh himself and, during Tutankhamun's reign, Horemheb and Ay, the men behind the throne. A similar, but not quite so powerful, position belonged to Amenhotep-Huy, who is described as the viceroy of the Egyptian lands in Kush, the part of Nubia conquered and held by Egypt during the 18th Dynasty. Amenhotep-Huy's wife is thought to have been called Taemwadjsi, who held the position of the head of Tutankhamun's harem. Unfortunately nothing else is known about this institution. We do not even know whether or not Tutankhamun had any other wives or concubines in addition to Ankhesenamun. The existence of a harem would tend to suggest that he did but the term can simply mean the members of his family and does not necessarily imply anything more than this. It is generally assumed that, because of his youth and because Ankhesenamun is the only royal woman depicted in his tomb, she was his only wife at the time of his death.

Everyday Objects

The superbly crafted and beautifully decorated ritual and funerary objects discovered in the tomb have received the bulk of the attention since it was opened by Howard Carter, but these were by no means the only artefacts found. There were a great many other items which generally have not received the attention they merit. In accordance with the Egyptian belief that a pharaoh who had died needed to take everything he would require for the afterlife with him during his journey through the underworld, a vast array of everyday items were placed in Tutankhamun's tomb. As these did not have the ritual or symbolic significance of the more decorative objects, many of them would have been the things Tutankhamun actually used on a daily basis.

A large quantity of pottery was found in the antechamber of the tomb, including bowls, cups and storage jars. Most of these pieces were undecorated, suggesting they were intended for everyday use. Stone and faience containers of various sorts were carefully packed in wooden boxes, including two pieces which look very much like teapots but were actually used in various religious libation ceremonies, such as the one known as the Opening of the Mouth. Residues found in some of the vessels indicated that they had been filled variously with oils, perfumes and cosmetics when they had been first placed in the tomb. Most had been opened on the two occasions the tomb was entered by robbers in antiquity, resulting in the contents decaying, but analysis of what was left was still possible. The robbers appear to have been disturbed before they could do any damage in the burial chamber and the treasury, which were found almost completely intact, but they rummaged through and scattered the contents of the antechamber and annex and, presumably, they removed some items. Only three glass cups were found, even though glass was manufactured on a relatively large scale during the 18th Dynasty. A wooden chest found by Howard Carter in the antechamber contained nothing but packing material, giving the impression it had been used to store fragile objects, possibly glass items, which were stolen by the robbers.

The tomb was also provisioned for the afterlife with a wide variety of food and drink. The nature of the foodstuffs found reflected the diet available to an ordinary Egyptian but there were also some luxury goods probably only affordable by a pharaoh or a member of the wealthy elite. A model of a granary, of a type which remained in use in Egypt until relatively recently, had been placed in the tomb. For those large items thought essential for the afterlife but which were too big to fit in the tomb, it was common practice to replace them with such models. The granary was divided into 16 compartments containing cereals, particularly emmer wheat and barley, the essential ingredients of Egyptian bread, and actual examples of the bread itself were also included. It also contained other staples of the Egyptian diet, such as chickpeas and lentils, and all the ingredients to make Egyptian beer, although not the actual beer itself. Egyptian beer, made to the consistency of a grainy soup or gruel, was much thicker than beer as we would recognise it today and it formed an important part of the Egyptian diet. Perhaps it was considered to be a drink for the masses rather than the pharaoh, or, perhaps, Tutankhamun simply did not have a taste for it, so it was not included.

A variety of baskets, made from dried grasses and palm leaves, contained fruit and vegetables, including onions, garlic, dates and dom palm fruit. Judging from the amount of jujubes, a fruit rather like dates grown in Egypt, this must have been particularly favoured by Tutankhamun. There were 36 baskets full of them in the tomb, along with jars of honey, almonds, coriander, cumin, fenugreek and a wide variety of other foods and ingredients. Ay, who is thought to have been responsible for putting together the grave goods, did not intend Tutankhamun to go hungry in the afterlife.

The single largest quantity of any food stuff was of meat. It was contained in 48 lozenge-shaped boxes which were stacked under a couch in the antechamber. The boxes were painted white on the outside and had a black resin spread on their interior surfaces. Most of them had been labelled with what should presumably have been the contents, but the dockets attached to each box rarely matched what was actually in them. It is not clear if the labelling had been done before the boxes had been filled, or if the person doing the labelling was in a hurry and was careless. Most of them contained cuts of beef, an expensive meat beyond the reach of most Egyptians, which showed the status of the pharaoh. There were also smaller numbers of geese and ducks, perhaps a favourite choice of Tutankhamun included to remind him of his hunting trips, although both were also kept domestically in Egypt. No meat from sheep or goats was found in the tomb, which would have been more readily available to the general population but may not have had the symbolic status of beef, the meat of the bull signifying the strength and virility of the pharaoh.

If Tutankhamun did not like beer, the same could not be said for wine. More than 30 wine jars were found in the tomb and recent research on the residues left in them has shown that they almost all contained red wine. Two types of jar were found; most were of the standard amphora design, having two handles and tapering almost to a point at the base, but there were also some of what are known as Syrian amphora. These have only one handle and resemble normal jugs except that they have rounded bottoms. Although described as Syrian, analysis of the clay used to make them showed that they were actually made locally. Many of the wine jars were labelled with similar information to that found on bottles of wine today, including the vintage, given as the regnal year of manufacture, the vineyard and the name of the wine maker. Much of the wine, labelled as coming from the House of Tutankhamun on the Western River, was from the pharaoh's own estates. The number of jars dating from the fourth and fifth years of Tutankhamun's reign indicate that these two years were particularly good vintages or, at least, that there had been bumper grape harvests in these years, leading to the production of a large quantity of wine. The ninth year was the last one to be represented, which can be taken as a sign that Tutankhamun died after the wine had been made from the grape harvest of that year but before the harvest of his tenth regnal year. Alternatively, of course, wine from the tenth year could simply have been of an inferior quality and so was not thought worthy of inclusion in the tomb.

Tutankhamun was provided with some entertainment to keep him amused in the afterlife. He appears to have liked playing board games, four examples of which were found in the tomb, although some of the pieces to go with the boards were missing. Two sets of the game senet were found, one built into a table and the other a smaller box which looks like a travelling version of the game. Each comprises of a board with 30 squares on it, arranged in three rows of ten. Unfortunately, the rules of the game are not known but it was played by two people and it seems as if the object was for a player to get his or her pieces through an S-shaped course on the board before the other person could.

Considering how popular music is thought to have been among the Egyptians, the number of musical instruments discovered in the tomb was relatively small. The instruments found had either a military function or were used in a religious context. The two trumpets found in the antechamber, one made of silver and the other of a copper alloy, were both of the type used by the Egyptian military for signalling, while ivory clappers and a pair of sistra, or hand-held rattles, were both used in religious ceremonies. It seems Tutankhamun was not a great music lover, or, perhaps, musical entertainment was thought to be already available in the afterlife so large numbers of instruments did not need to be included in the tomb.

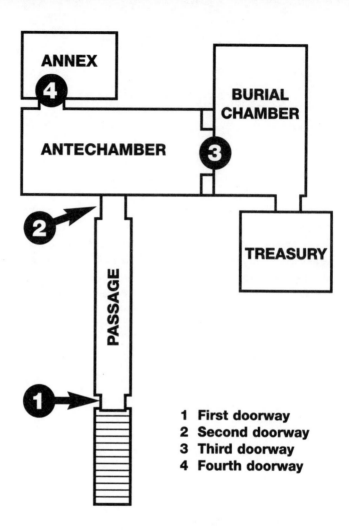

TUTANKHAMUN'S TOMB

(See page 90)

The Restoration of Amun

Religion in Egypt

Looked at from the standpoint of a secular western society, the religion of Egypt, with its huge pantheon of major and minor gods, is not easy to understand. Religion was inseparable from other aspects of the daily lives of Egyptians, providing an all-encompassing framework within which everything else occurred. Religious practices can be seen as being made up of two parts; the rituals and festivals associated with the state religion, with the semi-divine pharaoh at its head, and a personal religion which individuals practised as a means to gain the favour of the gods, thereby avoiding disaster and bad luck in their lives. But, for pharaohs and ordinary people alike, the gods were held to control everything that happened in the universe and, in order to gain their favour, people made offerings to them through the priesthoods of the temples.

This form of religion emerged very early in the history of Egypt, arising in the Neolithic agricultural communities along the banks of the Nile. As with farming peoples everywhere, their main concerns were with the continuation of the cycles of life and fertility which controlled their existence in an uncertain world. They recognised the mechanisms of the natural world which governed their lives: the annual flooding of the Nile, the changing of the seasons and the daily rising and setting of the sun. The failure of any of these, or an interruption of the cycles, would be disastrous for the production of food and for the people themselves.

The central tenet of belief involved preserving the order of the universe, as represented by the goddess Maat who, in Egyptian mythology, was brought into being at the moment of the creation, when order was formed out of chaos. The rising of the sun each morning represented a daily renewal of this order and, consequently, the sun god Ra was one of the most important of all the gods. When the sun went down in the evening, it entered the realm of the underworld, governed by the god Osiris, who guided the sun on a journey through his realm so that it could be reborn again in the morning. This belief was fundamental to the Egyptians and was central to the idea of rebirth and the afterlife. Ra and Osiris were linked together, as were life and death. Neither could exist without the other.

The gods were represented in human and animal forms, or in a combination of the two, and could have a range of associations which could change over time. New gods were constantly emerging and the characteristics of one god could merge with that of another. Some gods were worshipped throughout the country in major temples, while others were much more local, being worshipped in particular cities and religious centres or, even, in particular households.

During the 18th Dynasty, Amun, originally a local god of Thebes, rose in status to become one of the principal gods of the whole country. This can be attributed to the ascendancy of the Theban pharaohs to the throne of a reunited Egypt. In becoming a principal god, Amun came to be associated with Ra and his name was often written as Amun-Ra. The priesthood at Karnak also became much more powerful, with a large proportion of the total revenue of the entire country being expended on monumental building work at Karnak and on supporting the huge number of priests and attendant workers there. But, even though the various manifestations of the sun god were in the ascendancy, the other gods in the pantheon were not forgotten. To do so would be to invite their displeasure, which could have dire consequences for all the people of Egypt.

The Amarna Heresy

By the time of Amenhotep III, the sun god, always one of the main state gods, had come to be seen as the god from which all other gods had arisen. This process, known as henotheism, where a variety of gods begin to be seen as aspects of a central universal deity, can be seen as a development of religious practices throughout the 18th Dynasty, but it presented problems with the continued worship of the other gods in the pantheon who were now regarded as inferior to the sun god. The priesthood at Karnak had come to associate Amun with Ra, as Amun-Ra, and those at Heliopolis, the traditional centre of the worship of the sun god, began to merge Ra with a number of other gods, including Horus, under the title Ra-Horakhty. It was as if the two major religious centres in Egypt were competing with each other to promote their rival versions of the sun god. The priests at Karnak appeared to be winning the argument and became more powerful than those at Heliopolis. The Temple of Amun at Karnak steadily grew in size as successive pharaohs added their own monuments to it and it became the largest religious complex in the world at that time.

A theological problem arose during this process. How could one god become more important than all the other gods, and take on the aspects of many of these other gods, while these other gods continued to be worshipped and were thought to be essential for the continued well-being of the country? Amenhotep III attempted to resolve this problem by declaring himself divine during his own lifetime, as his father Thutmose IV may also have done, thereby setting himself on the same level as the other gods and declaring himself the son of the principal god. He particularly recognised the form of the sun god worshipped at Heliopolis, Ra-Horakhty, which included the actual body of the sun itself, the Aten or sun disc, as well as the various different gods associated with it. Late in his reign, he began to identify himself more closely with the Aten, giving himself the title 'the Dazzling Aten' and calling his palace in Thebes 'the House of the Dazzling Aten'. However, he does not seem to have resolved the problem entirely and he continued to associate himself with a number of other gods, including Amun, perhaps because the priesthood at Karnak had become too powerful to ignore.

Akhenaten's subsequent actions can be seen as the logical extension of what his father, and possibly his grandfather, before him had started. On coming to the throne, he instigated the construction of a temple at Karnak dedicated to Ra-Horakhty, represented in the same form as the god was in Heliopolis, with the body of a man and the head of a falcon. The full name of the god was extended to include the Aten, being written as 'Ra-Horakhty of the horizon who rejoices in the sunlight which is the Aten' and the hieroglyphs forming the name were enclosed in cartouches, as the names of pharaohs were. The Aten was being promoted as the King of the Gods and associated with the body of the pharaoh. It would not be long before Akhenaten shortened the name of the god to just that of the sun disc and began to worship the Aten to the exclusion of all the other gods. It is the first known example of a god being worshipped as an abstract manifestation of the divine, with no association with human or animal forms, and, as the Aten was the one and only god, some people have suggested this was also the first example of a monotheistic religion.

In the fifth year of his reign, Akhenaten began to build a new city on the west bank of the Nile in the middle of Egypt, about half way between Thebes and Memphis, at a site now known by its modern Egyptian name of el-Amarna. He called the new city Akhetaten, 'the Horizon of the Aten', and it was at about this time that he also changed his own name from the one he had been given at birth, Amenhotep, meaning 'Amun is Content', to the one by which he is generally known now, Akhenaten, 'the Glory of the Aten'. Nefertiti, which means 'the Beautiful One Has Come', also added Neferneferuaten, 'Beautiful is the Beauty of Aten', to her name at about the same time, which has been taken as a sign of her increasing importance in Akhenaten's court, where she took on many of the religious roles normally reserved for the pharaoh himself.

As well as a religious reason for moving (to establish a capital in the name of the Aten), there may also have been a very good political reason for the move to the new capital. It put a distance between Akhenaten and the Temple of Amun and its priesthood in Karnak, who had become so powerful that they may have been challenging the authority of the pharaoh. By proclaiming the Aten as the only god, Akhenaten was taking the power away from the Priesthood of Amun and concentrating it in himself. By moving away from Thebes to establish his own capital at Amarna, which also became the political and administrative centre of the country in place of Memphis, Akhenaten can be seen as taking actions to secure his own position and power base.

From inscriptions found on the boundary stelae at Amarna, it appears to have taken three or four years for building work to have progressed enough for Akhenaten to move his family and court to the city. He was certainly living there by the ninth year of his reign and the move appears to have allowed him to become much more radical as a politician and religious leader. Freed from the restraints imposed on him by the proximity of the Priesthood of Amun, he issued a royal decree banning the worship of all gods other than the Aten. Temples were closed down across the country, the images of the other gods were destroyed and their names removed from monuments, and the many festivals dedicated to the other gods, particularly Amun, were prohibited. An operation of this size could only have been carried out with the cooperation and active participation of the Egyptian army, the only organisation which could have been mobilised throughout the country to carry out Akhenaten's decrees in the face of what must surely have been fierce opposition from the priesthoods.

The iconography of the Aten was also a radical departure from the traditional Egyptian representations of their gods. The human and animal forms of representation were abolished and the Aten was shown solely as the disc of the sun with its rays reaching out from it and ending in human hands. Images of Akhenaten and Nefertiti were shown under the rays of the Aten, as if being held in its protective care. Akhenaten was represented in pictures and statues in a very different form from that of any previous pharaoh, shown as an almost androgynous figure with protruding breasts and feminine hips. He was depicted with an elongated head, a protruding chin and thick lips, large almond-shaped eyes and a bulging stomach, giving rise to suggestions that, if these representations were in any way accurate, he must have been suffering from some form of genetic disease, although there is no hard evidence to support such a theory. These strange representations which, according to an inscription left by one of the sculptors, were done on the orders of the pharaoh himself, were more likely to have been an expression of his religious beliefs. Some modern art critics have described this new style as being expressionist in form and, at times, almost verging on the surrealist.

The physical form of the pharaoh was not the only departure from the art that had gone before. For the first time in Egyptian history, the pharaoh was shown in relaxed and intimate scenes with his wife and daughters. A stele found during the excavation of a house in Amarna, and now in the Altes Museum in Berlin, shows Akhenaten and Nefertiti seated under the rays of the Aten, playing with three of their daughters. The scene is like a family portrait, with the children crawling over their parents, although it is thought to have been part of a shrine and may well actually represent Akhenaten and his family as divine. Even if this was the case, the art has none of the rigidity and formality of previous depictions of pharaohs which, as was usual in all Egyptian art before the Amarna period, were set out on an unvarying grid pattern. Amarna art became much more fluid and dynamic, depicting Akhenaten and Nefertiti in natural poses and giving the impression of movement and speed. The majority of the changes made by Akhenaten would not last but this more relaxed style of art was one of the few to continue after his death.

The revolutionary new style in art was also apparent in the architecture of the temples built at Amarna. The main building materials used for their construction were mud bricks, rather than the more usual large blocks of quarried stone. No doubt this allowed building work to proceed much more quickly than it had in the past, but it would also make the temples easier to demolish when attempts were made to destroy all references to Akhenaten after his death. The temples were open to the sun, allowing the rays of the Aten to penetrate throughout the interior of the building. It was in stark contrast to the standard design of temples, which had small dark enclosed inner sanctuaries, where the icons of the god of the temples were kept and to which only the most senior priests were allowed admittance.

This is not to say that Akhenaten's temples were any more egalitarian than previous temples had been. If anything, they were even more exclusive. The royal family alone was allowed to perform the rituals in the temples in Amarna. This could have been a reflection of Akhenaten's opinion about his own divinity, seeing himself and Nefertiti as the sole links between the mortal and the Aten, to the exclusion of any priests. In this respect, it can be seen as a further reaction against the power previously attached to the priesthood in temples. By restricting contact with the Aten to himself and his family,

Akhenaten was continuing the process of concentrating power in his own hands.

Akhenaten left a record of his beliefs in the form of the Hymn to the Aten, which is thought to have been composed by the pharaoh himself. The most complete known example of the hymn was found in the unused Amarna tomb of Ay, who was a senior member of Akhenaten's court before going on to serve Tutankhamun and eventually gaining the throne himself. Ay was actually buried in a tomb in the Valley of the Kings and the tomb in Amarna was abandoned before it was finished, but not before the hymn had been inscribed on the walls. It sets out Akhenaten's belief in the Aten as the only god, who created the world and everything in it, and lists some of the creator's achievements. In the hymn, Akhenaten also identifies himself as the son of the one and only god. Similarities between the hymn and Psalm 104 have been recognised, although whether the hymn had a direct influence on the composition of the psalm or if they were independently expressing similar religious concerns is not known. It is one strand of evidence used by some academics to support the theory of a cultural link between the religion of Akhenaten and Judaism.

Akhenaten's own tomb was also in Amarna, cut into the cliff face of what is now known as the Royal Wadi. In yet another break from tradition, the site of the tomb is on the east bank of the Nile, on the side of the rising sun, symbolising life, rather than on the west bank of the river, the usual location of burial sites. Much of the decoration of the tomb, which was discovered in the late nineteenth century, was defaced in the immediate aftermath of the Amarna Period and the sarcophagus in the tomb was found smashed into numerous pieces, although it has since been reconstructed and now stands in the car park of the Egyptian Museum in Cairo. Rather than being decorated in the usual manner, with the images of the four protective goddesses, Isis, Nephthys, Neith and Selkis, at each corner, Akhenaten's sarcophagus was protected by four figures of Nefertiti. There were no representations of Osiris, the god of the underworld, anywhere in the tomb, which was not only an indication of Akhenaten's proscription of all other gods but a rejection of death. Akhenaten, according to his own theology, would live forever in the light of the Aten.

The Beginning of the End

At its height, the population of the city established by Akhenaten at Amarna could have been as high as 50,000 but, within a few short years of his death, the city was completely abandoned. This represented a complete reversal of the religious reforms initiated by Akhenaten and a return to the older form of worship and the pantheon of gods. One of the outcomes of the reformation was an attempt by Akhenaten's successors to wipe his name from history by destroying everything he had built, including the city, and removing his name from all the inscriptions carved during his lifetime. One of the results of this has been to make it all but impossible to discover how Akhenaten's radical theological experiment came to an end. One of the most likely reasons for the failure is that Akhenaten lost the support of the general population, who found his new religion to be elitist and inaccessible.

It is difficult to say to what extent the religious changes implemented by Akhenaten were actually adopted by the wider population of Egypt. Access to the major gods had always been controlled by the state and the priesthood and the only occasions when ordinary people could interact directly with these gods would have been during religious festivals, when icons of the gods were brought out of the inner sanctuaries of the temples and carried through the streets in processions. By banning all of the gods except the Aten, Akhenaten put an end to these religious festivals, together with the practice of making offerings to the gods at temples. The effect of this was to severely limit the religious practices of the majority of the people and it seems probable that many would have deeply resented this. It was an enormous change in the daily lives of ordinary people, who suddenly found the gods they relied on to bring good fortune into their lives banned and replaced by a god to whom they had virtually no access at all.

Excavations of houses of ordinary people in Amarna have uncovered private shrines and idols dedicated to other gods as well as to the Aten so, even in Amarna, Akhenaten's reforms were not universally accepted. It is difficult to date finds in other parts of the country accurately enough to know for certain whether or not the old religion continued alongside the reformed religion but it is safe to assume that, if Akhenaten's prohibitions were not being explicitly followed in the centre of Atenism, then the rest of the country did not unconditionally accept the changes either. The worship of the old gods did not die out, but may have been driven underground, with people maintaining their beliefs in the privacy of their own homes.

Essentially what Akhenaten was demanding of his people was the abandonment of their personal beliefs. He was the

Son of God and, as such, the devotion of the people had to be directed through him. The pharaoh had always held an exalted position but, under Akhenaten, the prosperity and well-being of all the inhabitants of Egypt became his personal responsibility. This was all very well while the country remained wealthy and the people happy and healthy, as appears to have been the case at the start of Akhenaten's reign, but, as soon as anything went wrong, people would quickly turn against him. It is speculation to suggest that this is what happened to Akhenaten but, based on the available evidence, it is not beyond the realms of possibility either.

Towards the end of Akhenaten's reign, he appears to have encountered a number of personal and political setbacks which could have triggered a popular movement against him. Decorations in his tomb in the Royal Wadi show him and Nefertiti mourning the death of at least one of their daughters. There are some suggestions that Nefertiti herself also died at about the same time, although she may simply have changed her name as part of the process of becoming co-regent with Akhenaten. Evidence from excavations carried out in burial grounds in a number of different parts of Egypt shows a sudden increase in the number of burials from this period. The people who were dying came from a wider cross section of society than would normally be expected in such burials, where the majority of deaths would be of the very old and the very young. This suggests there was a serious outbreak of an epidemic, possibly even the black plague, towards the end of Akhenaten's reign, which could have caused the deaths of about 20 per cent of the entire population of the country. In the light of the abandonment of the old gods and of Akhenaten's personal responsibility for the country's well-being, such an outbreak could, at the very least, result in people thinking the epidemic had been caused by the pharaoh offending the old gods. A logical extension of this would be for demands to be made for an end to the exclusive worship of the Aten and for a return to the old ways, when people could make offerings to the gods themselves to ensure their own personal safety.

Diplomatic Relations

An accusation often levelled at Akhenaten is that, while he was concentrating on making revolutionary changes within Egypt, he was neglecting the rest of the empire and diplomatic relations with countries beyond its borders. The Amarna letters, a cache of diplomatic correspondence from Egyptian vassal states and allies in the Levant and Syria, has shed some light on the situation. The letters themselves were found in the remains of a building known as the House of Correspondence of the Pharaoh in Amarna in the late nineteenth century and are now scattered among a number of different museums around the world. There are something like 400 of them and they were sent to Egypt over a period of about 20 or 30 years, initially to Amenhotep III, then to Akhenaten and finally to Tutankhamun during the short time he remained in Amarna after becoming pharaoh. Most of the letters found were copies of the original letters made by scribes. They were written in Akkadian, the language of the Assyrians and Babylonians which was used as the common language of diplomacy at the time, and were in the cuneiform script, a form of writing developed by the Sumerians and common to much of the Near East.

Both the content and chronology of the letters have proved to be a source of intense debate in the academic world but, even so, they give a picture of the Amarna Period somewhat at odds with the conventional view that Akhenaten ignored foreign relations. Although the Egyptian side of the correspondence was not included in the archive, the extent of the letters and the number of different states represented suggests Akhenaten was deeply concerned with what was going on outside Egypt and the empire. What the letters appear to show is an increase in disagreements and fighting between various vassal states, together with a greater threat from outside the empire, particularly from the emerging Hittite Empire to the north, which was perhaps attempting to exploit the infighting of the vassal states for its own ends.

The most frequent letter writer was Ribaddi (sometimes transliterated as Rib-Hadda), the king of the city state of Byblos, an important trading port on the coast of what is now Lebanon, north of Beirut, which had been a close trading partner with Egypt over a long period of time, particularly in the supply of the timber of the cedars of Lebanon for ship building. Ribaddi wrote about 60 letters to Akhenaten, complaining about his neighbouring states and requesting urgent military assistance to prevent the invasion of Byblos. He appears to have had constant problems with Abdi-Ashrta, the king of Amurru, a state to the west of Byblos, who was intent on expanding his sphere of influence and, no doubt, recognised the importance of adding a wealthy trading port to his territory. Although we do not know exactly what was in Akhenaten's replies to the repeated entreaties for assistance, he appeared to be offering no support. Perhaps he was content to let the rival states fight it out amongst themselves.

At one point he was apparently growing tired of the constant barrage of complaints and demands, telling Ribaddi to stop bothering him all the time.

Ribaddi wrote to Akhenaten to tell him Abdi-Ashrta had been killed, but his son Aziru continued the campaign. Aziru eventually captured Byblos and handed Ribaddi to the ruler in the rival port of Siddon, where it is highly likely he was killed. Akhenaten does not appear to have been pleased by this, even though he had not done anything to stop it, and he summoned Aziru to Egypt to explain his actions. After Aziru had been in Egypt for a year, Akhenaten received reports of the Hittites advancing on Amurru and he allowed Aziru to return to his kingdom to defend his territory. Once Aziru got there, he entered into talks with the Hittite king Suppiluliuma I and switched allegiance to the Hittites, handing control of a strategically important region of the Egyptian Empire's northern border to its main rivals.

The Amarna Letters contain a number of reports on the activities of the Hittites. Unfortunately, because the chronology of the letters is difficult to establish, it is hard to know exactly when they were threatening the northern borders of the Egyptian Empire. The letters from the king of the Mitanni, offering one of his daughters as a wife to Akhenaten, can be interpreted as the cementing of an alliance between Egypt and the Mitanni, perhaps made in the hope of seeing off the threat of the Hittites. If this was the case, it clearly did not work. By year twelve of Akhenaten's reign, the Hittites had defeated the Mitanni, leaving them free to move against Egypt's vassal states in northern Syria.

The threat of a Hittite invasion was not the only problem Akhenaten was facing. In the same year an Egyptian army was sent to Nubia to put down a rebellion, and this seems to have been successfully achieved. Perhaps this was the reason why Akhenaten was not more supportive of the northern vassal states. The army was busy in the south, protecting Egypt's economically vital territory in Nubia, where the gold mines that underwrote Egypt's wealth were situated. At the same time the army had to continue to implement Akhenaten's unpopular reforms at home. It is speculation to say that the army was becoming overstretched and, as a result, dissatisfied with the rule of Akhenaten. However, if this was the case, and Akhenaten was also losing the support of the general population and the priesthood, then his continued reign as pharaoh was becoming untenable.

The Restoration

The details of Akhenaten's death and the immediate aftermath of the succession to the throne are entirely unknown. He died during the seventeenth year of his reign and, within a year or two of his death, Tutankhamun, probably Akhenaten's only living male relative, was made pharaoh at the age of eight or nine. With the empire apparently threatened on two fronts, by the Hittites and by the Nubians, with Egypt suffering from the effects of a terrible epidemic and with the general population turning against the reforms Akhenaten had instituted, it was hardly a good moment for such a young boy to become the supreme leader of the country. Perhaps he was installed by the powerful elite, including Horemheb and Ay, who controlled the court, as a figurehead behind which they could continue to run the country. Tutankhamun could have represented both a fresh start and a return to the values of the previous pharaohs, before Akhenaten. If the people of Egypt were looking back to a golden age during the reigns of Thutmose IV and Amenhotep III, when the wealth of the nation had reached its greatest heights and there was relative peace along its borders, a ruler from the same blood line could, perhaps, be seen as a means to return to it.

The problem with such a scenario is that Tutankhamun was also closely associated with Akhenaten. Tutankhamun's advisers needed to dissociate the new pharaoh from his father and all he stood for. On this occasion there is actually some primary source material to support this line of speculation. Often described as the most important document remaining from Tutankhamun's reign (actually, it has to be since it is pretty much the only one), the Restoration Stele contains an inscription concerning the terrible state of the country at the start of Tutankhamun's reign and what the new pharaoh proposed to do about it.

The stele, now in the Egyptian Museum in Cairo, is a slab of red granite, about 8 feet 4 inches (2.5m) high. It was found in an excavation conducted at the Great Temple of Amun at Karnak in 1905. The place where it was found is significant, assuming it had not been moved there from where it was originally erected. It stood in front of the Third Pylon, a massive ceremonial gateway erected by Amenhotep III, in a prominent and highly visible position right in front of the temple as it was in Tutankhamun's day. Anybody coming to the temple could not fail to see it or miss what must have been the intentional association with Amenhotep III.

The text begins with Tutankhamun's full five-part name. At some point Tutankhamun's praenomen and nomen were chiselled out and replaced with those of Horemheb. Considering

Tutankhamun would have been about ten years old when the text of the stele was written, it is entirely possible that Horemheb had a hand in its composition and, on ascending to the throne, wanted to claim it for himself. Unfortunately for him, whoever made the changes did not do a particularly thorough job, as Tutankhamun's name remains legible under the new inscription and, in any case, his identity can easily be established from the other three names which were not defaced at all.

The main body of the text is given below:

The good god, son of Amun, son of Kamutef [a reference to Horus], the good son, the holy egg created by Amun, father of the Two Lands, the one who makes the one who made him, the ba [the spirit or soul] of Heliopolis united in order to form him, to be king forever, as Horus, living immortally. He is the effective king who did what was good for his father and all the gods. He restored everything that was ruined to be his monument forever. He has vanquished chaos from the whole land and has restored Maat to her place. He has made lying a crime, the whole land being made as it was at the time of creation.

Now when His Majesty was crowned king the temples and estates of the gods and goddesses from Elephantine as far as the marshes of Lower Egypt had fallen into ruin. Their shrines had fallen down, turned into piles of rubble and overgrown with weeds. Their sanctuaries were as if they had never existed at all. Their temples had become footpaths. The world was in chaos and the gods had turned their backs on this land. If an army was sent to Djahy [thought to be in Syria] to extend the boundaries of Egypt, it would have no success. If you asked a god for advice he would not attend to you and if you spoke to a goddess she would not listen either. Hearts were faint in bodies because everything that had been was destroyed.

Now some days after His Majesty appeared upon the throne of his father and he ruled the Two Banks of Horus [all of Egypt], the Black Land [the Nile valley and Delta] and the Red Land [the desert] were under his authority and every land bowed down before his might. His Majesty was in his palace which was in the House of Aakheperkare [referring to Tutankhamun's ancestry going back to Thutmose I], being like the sun in the sky, and His Majesty carried out the works of this land and everything the Two Lands needed every day. Then His Majesty considered in his heart and looked for something which would be effective for his father Amun. He made the holy statue out of genuine electrum [an alloy of gold and silver], giving to it more than he had done before. He made his father Amun thirteen poles long, the holy statue being made of electrum, lapis lazuli, turquoise and every noble and precious stone, although the majesty of this noble god had been only seven poles long before. His Majesty made monuments for the gods, making their statues of electrum from the tribute of the foreign lands. He renewed their sanctuaries as his monuments forever, endowing them with offerings forever, laying aside for them divine offerings daily, laying aside bread from the earth. He added great wealth on top of that which existed before, doing more than his predecessors had ever done. He allocated waab priests [local lay priests in a temple], God's servants and the heirs of the Chiefs of the Cities, to be the sons of wise men whose reputation is established. He has enriched their tables with gold and silver, bronze and copper without limit. He has filled their storehouses with male and female workers and with His Majesty's booty. He has added to the wealth of every temple, doubling, trebling and quadrupling the silver, gold, lapis lazuli, turquoise and every noble and precious stone, together with byssus [very fine linen], white linen, ordinary linen, oil, fat, resin, incense, perfumes and myrrh without limit.

(From the transliteration by Benedict G. Davies in *Egyptian Historical Research of the Eighteenth Dynasty v6*, Aris and Philips [1995]).

The text is a repudiation of Akhenaten's reign, without actually mentioning his name, and the disastrous state he left the country in when he died. Tutankhamun was being associated with Amun and the other gods and goddesses in the Egyptian pantheon, including Maat, who represented the divine order of the universe. Out of the chaos that preceded him, the text claims, Tutankhamun had restored the prestige of the crown and the overall prosperity of the country. He rebuilt the temples across the whole country, in contrast, no doubt, to Akhenaten concentrating all his efforts and tax revenue on building work in Amarna, and had appointed the right people to the priesthoods of the restored temples to administer to the needs of the people through the rituals of making offerings to the gods and conducting the required festivals and processions. Without saying it in so many words, Tutankhamun is telling the people of Egypt that the pharaoh is no longer the only conduit to the gods, as Akhenaten had claimed, and that they were free to worship as they pleased.

As with all primary source material, attention has to be paid to the context. The country was apparently facing a crisis and Tutankhamun was being set up as the solution to the problem. The gods had turned their backs on the people but, under Tutankhamun, they were being appeased with offerings and the restoration of the temples. How much of this is propaganda, or spin as we might call it now, and how much is a factual account of what was really happening is impossible to tell, but the message is clear – the mistakes of the past are behind us and we can look forward to a brighter future.

Evidence that the text of the Restoration Stele was more than just words comes from the amount of building work carried out across the country during Tutankhamun's reign. Maya, who was in charge of the treasury in Tutankhamun's administration, appears to have travelled throughout the country to supervise the restoration of old temples and the building of new ones. It can be seen as the new pharaoh making the restoration of the old gods obvious to the Egyptian people across the whole country. They could see with their own eyes that the restoration was really happening as the building work continued. Alongside this, work was also being done publicly to erase the memory of Akhenaten by removing his name from inscriptions and by demolishing the temples dedicated to Aten he had built. The demolition work began in Thebes, with much of the rubble being reused in the construction work at the temples in Karnak and Luxor, and continued throughout the country, including in Amarna, which would cease to exist entirely over the course of the next few decades.

Although the evidence is by no means conclusive, Maya

may also have been responsible for removing the bodies of the royal family from the Royal Wadi in Amarna and reburying them in the Valley of the Kings. The tomb designated as KV55 contained various pieces of evidence to suggest that it had been used to house the mummies of Akhenaten and Tiye, the wife of Amenhotep III. A mummy, thought to be that of a man, was actually found in the tomb when it was first opened in 1907 and was identified by some scholars as that of Akhenaten, although it is now thought to be Smenkhare's.

Moving the royal mummies from Amarna to the Valley of the Kings suggests that Tutankhamun had not forgotten about his family, even though he went along with the restoration of Amun and the repudiation of Akhenaten. A few items found in his tomb would tend to support this idea. A lock of hair was found in a nest of four small coffins which carried an inscription identifying it as being from the head of Tiye, Akhenaten's mother and, in all probability, Tutankhamun's grandmother. She outlived Amenhotep III by something like 12 years and accompanied her son to Amarna, becoming, as described by some, the matriarch of the royal family in the Amarna Period. Other items in the tomb were inscribed with the names of Akhenaten himself, Neferneferuaten (the name adopted by Nefertiti during her co-regency with Akhenaten), and Mekketaten and Meritaten, the two eldest daughters of Akhenaten and Nefertiti. It is possible that these items were actually taken from the desecrated royal tombs in Amarna specifically to be used as grave goods for Tutankhamun but, wherever they came from, they provide an intriguing picture of a Tutankhamun who was not as committed to the changes occurring during his reign as the Restoration Stele makes out.

Death of a Pharaoh

An Unexpected Death

In one of the more widely accepted chronologies of the Egyptian pharaohs, Tutankhamun is said to have died in 1327 BC, during the ninth, or possibly tenth, year of his reign. This broadly agrees with Manetho, who stated that the pharaoh died in his ninth regnal year, assuming, as appears entirely likely, the pharaoh he names as Rathosis is actually Tutankhamun. The presence of wine jars in his tomb bearing labels dating them to the ninth regnal year would suggest Tutankhamun died quite late in that year, certainly after the grape harvest and the wine-making process had been finished. A garland of flowers had been placed around his coffin during the funeral, presumably shortly before the sarcophagus was closed, and the type of flowers used, including cornflowers and mandrake, bloom in Egypt in late March. A number of different fresh fruits which also ripen in the same month, including dates and jujubes, were also placed in the tomb, so it would be reasonable to say that the funeral took place at this time of year.

Given that mummification was a ceremonial process intended to take 70 days to complete, following the guidelines set out in the funerary texts of the period, an approximate date of death can be given as January 1327 BC. There are some indications that Tutankhamun may have died earlier than this and the funeral was delayed, perhaps because the tomb was not ready at the time of his death or because the issue of the succession had to be sorted out before the funeral could take place. If this was the case, then the date of death would be at some point towards the end of 1326 BC. This is supported to a certain extent by allusions to the death of a pharaoh found in a contemporary archive of documents in the Hittite capital of Hattusa. An Egyptian king is said to have died in the late summer and, although the documents do not definitely identify the person to whom they are referring, there are indications that it is Tutankhamun.

The tomb itself gives the impression of having been prepared in a hurry. As extensive as the grave goods are, running in total to over 5,000 items, many appear to have been recycled from other tombs, particularly those of the royal family from the Amarna period. As Tutankhamun's tomb is the only one of the 26 tombs of pharaohs to have been found in the Valley of the Kings still containing the majority of its grave goods, the others all having been robbed in antiquity, it is impossible to know if this was a common practice or if it was specific to Tutankhamun. Considering the great wealth of the pharaohs of this period, it would be reasonable to assume that grave goods were recycled for the sake of convenience rather than necessity or, as in Tutankhamun's case, because there was simply not enough time to assemble the materials for the tomb without using goods from other tombs.

The recycled grave goods are not the only indication of a hastily arranged funeral. The main body of Tutankhamun's sarcophagus was carved out of a single block of a golden yellow quartzite, but the lid was of red granite and had been painted yellow in an attempt to make it match. It had also been broken in half at some stage and, rather than being replaced, was repaired with gypsum plaster, giving the impression that there was not enough time to start again and make a new one. Previous inscriptions on the sarcophagus had been chipped away and new ones relating to Tutankhamun added, suggesting it had been made originally for somebody else and then recycled for Tutankhamun. The features of one of the three anthropoid coffins, which were placed inside each other in the manner of Russian dolls, bore little resemblance to those of the other two, again giving the impression that it had not been originally made for Tutankhamun.

The decoration on the walls of the tomb were quite roughly done compared to other royal tombs, as if the artists were working to a strict timetable, and the tomb itself was, by the standards of other royal tombs in the Valley of the Kings, small and insignificant. It was more like the tombs built for the elite and members of the court who had been given the honour of a burial in the royal necropolis, rather than those built for a pharaoh. This has led to suggestions that the tomb, KV62 in the classification system of tombs in the Valley of the Kings, was not the one originally intended for him. Another tomb, KV23, has been suggested as the one built for Tutankhamun, but either it was not completed in time or it was taken over by Ay, Tutankhamun's successor.

Tomb building for a pharaoh, tunnelling into the limestone walls of the Valley of the Kings with tools made from stone, copper and bronze, took a great deal of time and effort, so it was usually started as soon as the pharaoh came to power.

Tutankhamun died in his ninth or tenth regnal year, which allowed plenty of time to build a much more elaborate tomb than KV62. One possible explanation is that, because the intended tomb was still under construction when he died, then he was buried in KV62. The plan was to move him to KV23 when it was finished but, after Ay came to power, he changed his mind and adopted Tutankhamun's tomb for himself. Whatever the truth of the matter, every indication points towards Tutankhamun dying suddenly, leaving his court and officials unprepared to give him a funeral on the scale they would usually have done for a pharaoh.

Forensic investigations of the mummy tend to confirm this theory. No sign of any long term illness or life-threatening disability have been found. An X-ray carried out on the body in 1968 showed some abnormalities, including a slight curvature of the spine, which was interpreted at the time as evidence that Tutankhamun was disabled during his lifetime. Several depictions of him found in the tomb show him sitting down, even when he is hunting ducks with a bow and arrow, and there are also a number of scenes of him holding what appears to be a walking stick in his hand. This has been presented as further evidence of a disability, but there are many more scenes of him involved in physical activities which cannot be interpreted in this way, including ones of him standing unaided and hunting from the back of a chariot, indicating he was physically healthy. A CT scan was carried out in 2005, from which a three-dimensional image of the mummy has been produced which shows the tissue as well as the bones of the skeleton, and this showed that the abnormalities within the body, including the curved spine, were almost certainly caused either during the mummification process or when

Howard Carter and his team removed the body from its coffin.

Indications are, then, that Tutankhamun's death was unexpected. He was a young man who, according to the CT scan, was in good health in the years leading up to his death. Suggestions made in the past that he was a sickly and weak child or that he suffered from some form of congenital disease appear to be wrong. This does, of course, beg the question – how did Tutankhamun die?

Accidental Death or Murder?

When a young man dies suddenly and unexpectedly, with no sign of any medical reason for his death, there are really only two possible explanations. Either he died as the result of an accident or he was killed. Regicide makes for a much more sensational headline than accidental death, so it is hardly surprising to find many accounts of Tutankhamun's life stressing the likelihood that he was killed in suspicious circumstances. But does the evidence really point to murder or is this more a case of modern authors adapting the evidence to fit the story they would like to tell?

In the 1968 X-ray, a dark spot showed up on the inside of the skull at the back of Tutankhamun's head. A fragment of bone was also found to be loose inside the cranium and, together, these were taken as evidence of a subdural haematoma, caused by a heavy blow to the back of the head. Although there was no way of knowing if any blow received by Tutankhamun had been intentional or the result of an accident, the X-ray was interpreted by many as proof that Tutankhamun was murdered. In any homicide case the ensuing investigation focuses on the motive of the murderer and, in Tutankhamun's case, the most obvious motive for killing him was so that the killer could benefit from his wealth and power. Ay, the man who succeeded him to the throne, had the most to gain from his death and so became the chief suspect. He was one of Tutankhamun's chief advisors, perhaps acting in the role of regent while Tutankhamun was too young to govern for himself. When Tutankhamun came of age, one theory suggests, Ay either murdered him or had him killed so he could become pharaoh in Tutankhamun's place. The only problem with this theory is that the two strands of evidence used to support it, the presence of the dark spot on the inside of the skull and the bone fragment, can be more convincingly explained as the result of actions occurring after Tutankhamun had died rather than as the cause of his death.

As part of the mummification process Tutankhamun's embalmers would have removed his brain, using a special tool to extract it through his nose, and then filled the brain cavity with a resinous embalming fluid. Assuming the body was lying on its back while this was being done, as would be expected, the fluid would have collected at the back of the skull, where it would have subsequently dried and solidified as a black resin, which is what showed up in the X-ray. If the bone fragment had been inside the skull after the brain had been removed, then surely it would have become stuck in the embalming fluid after this was introduced into the cavity in the embalming process. The fragment probably became detached from the skull after the embalming process had been completed, not as a result of a blow to the head. The most likely explanation is that the fragment was dislodged from the skull either when the mummy was removed from its coffin by Howard Carter and his team or while it was being unwrapped. The methods used to do this were, to say the least, crude. The mummy was firmly stuck to the coffin by resin from the embalming process and the various substances used in the libation ceremonies of the funeral. Carter's team used hot knives to melt the resin and then cut the mummy out of its coffins. During the unwrapping, they appear to have paid more attention to recovery of the various items of jewellery which had been placed within the bandages by the embalmers than to the preservation of the body. In order to remove all the jewellery which adorned the body itself, it was extensively dismembered, causing serious damage to the embalmed tissue and skeleton. During this process the head was completely severed from the body and it was at this moment, more than likely, that the fragment of bone was broken.

The Egyptian team who conducted the CT scan in 2005, led by Dr Zahi Hawass, found no evidence of a blow to the back of the head, accidental or otherwise. They did discover a compound fracture of the left femur just above the knee, which they concluded was not broken during Carter's dismemberment of the body. There were a number of other breakages in various bones that had clearly been caused by Carter and his men, but the ends of the bones in these cases had sharp edges, showing they had been cut or sawn through. The edges of the bone of the leg fracture were jagged, consistent with a break caused by a fall from some height. Embalming fluid was also found on the jagged edges of the bone, showing it was broken prior to the start of the embalming process. This does not rule out the possibility that the embalmers themselves broke the bone but there was no reason to do so in order to mummify the body and so it would seem unlikely. There were no clear signs of any healing of the broken bone or the wound caused by the compound fracture, leading the team to put forward the hypothesis that Tutankhamun died shortly after breaking his leg, probably within a few days. The injury, although severe, was not, in itself, necessarily life-threatening. The cause of death, according to the team, would more likely have been a secondary infection of the wound in the leg, such as gangrene or septicaemia.

The CT scan came up with a number of other interesting results. It confirmed the findings of the earlier X-ray which showed that Tutankhamun's sternum and most of the front of his rib cage were missing. The sharp edges of the rib bones suggest they have been cut away at some point, possibly by the embalmers. This has led to a theory that Tutankhamun's rib cage was crushed at the same time as his leg was broken but, because any evidence of broken ribs has been removed, this is impossible to confirm. Dr Hawass considers it to be unlikely since the embalmers, had they removed the sternum and ribs, would have placed them in the tomb along with the internal organs and other bodily remains removed during the embalming process. These internal organs were found by Carter and had been placed in so-called canopic jars in a shrine in the tomb but the sternum and ribs were not present. The only other possibility is that Carter's team removed the sternum and ribs during their forensic examination of the body, although what possible reason they could have for doing this remains a mystery. Hawass suggests they were attempting to remove beads hanging round Tutankhamun's neck, although damaging the body to that extent and then not mentioning they had done so in their report would be highly negligent in a supposedly scientific examination.

As well as the broken leg and possible damage to the ribs, Tutankhamun had a deep cut, going down to the bone, on his left cheek. The cut had hardly healed at all, so it must have occurred shortly before he died, possibly at the same time as he broke his leg. The nature of the cut is consistent with it being caused by a sharp blade of some kind, but it is not possible to be certain if it was made by a knife or an arrow. One scenario, taking into account all three injuries, involves Tutankhamun being hit in the face by a sharp object while driving his chariot, either during a hunt or on a military campaign. This caused him to fall out of the chariot and he was then hit by another one following close behind, which resulted in the breaking of his leg and the crushing of his chest. In reality, this simply replaces one speculative theory – that Tutankhamun was murdered by Ay – with another, but this one does have the advantage of being based on all the latest available evidence.

Other information arising from the scan includes confirmation that Tutankhamun had a highly elongated skull, thought to have been a family trait rather than the result of a congenital disease. A mummy found in tomb KV55 showed a remarkable similarity to Tutankhamun in this respect and it has been informally identified as that of Smenkhare, who could have been his older brother. Analysis of the blood of the two mummies showed they also shared the same blood group when tested for two different antigens, on the ABO and MNS systems. Both were A2 and MN on these two systems and, while this is not proof they came from the same family, it provides an indication of a possible relationship.

The scan showed that Tutankhamun was probably taller than had previously been thought, being about 5 feet 11 inches (1.80m), and that he was approximately 19 years old at the time of his death. His teeth were in a good overall condition, but he had an impacted wisdom tooth, which could well have caused him some pain, and a pronounced overbite, another trait probably shared with other members of his family. The team also found evidence that Tutankhamun had a cleft palette, although they did not think it was serious enough to have shown up as a hare lip.

The Egyptian Way of Death

Although they were probably not as obsessed as they can sometimes appear, the Ancient Egyptians, at least to modern eyes, did spend an inordinate amount of time making preparations for death and the afterlife. A large proportion of the archaeological evidence uncovered in Egypt has a funerary or, at least, a religious context, highlighting these aspects of life rather than the more mundane ones. One reason for this is that the Egyptian elites, and in particular the pharaohs, really did put a large amount of time and effort into making preparations for the afterlife by constructing elaborate tombs and mortuary temples in stone which were intended to last for eternity. By contrast, most houses and other buildings were made from mud bricks and they have not survived in the archaeological record. Another reason is that Egyptologists have, over the years, concentrated their efforts on tombs and temples, where the most exciting discoveries are likely to be made, and have, until relatively recently, not been inclined to study the everyday life of the wider population.

The knowledge of Egyptian beliefs about death and burial gained through archaeology has been greatly enhanced by the various funerary texts found in tombs. The best known of these is the Book of the Dead, a collection of spells which was placed in tombs to help the dead negotiate their way through the underworld. Spell 125, perhaps the best-known part of the book, details the judgement of Osiris, where the hearts of the dead are weighed against a feather of an ostrich, which represents Maat, the goddess of order and justice. According to the book, if the dead failed the test and were deemed unfit to progress into the afterlife, because they had committed evil deeds in their lives, their hearts were consumed by Ammut, the devourer of the dead, a fabulous creature of the underworld made up of the head of a crocodile, the front of a lion and the back end of a hippopotamus. Those who passed the test were led by Osiris into the afterlife, sometimes represented as an agricultural paradise called the Field of Reeds.

Egyptian funerary practices, and religion in general, changed and developed over time. Death, together with life, was considered to be an integral part of a cycle, in which neither was possible without the other. In life people passed through the realm of Ra, the sun god, and, once they died, they transferred to the underworld, governed by Osiris. The blessed dead, those who had passed the judgement of Maat, embarked on a journey from one realm to another, passing through a transitional or liminal zone which had to be safely navigated in order to attain the afterlife. Placing a dead body into the ground, in a grave or a tomb, was symbolically giving the body back to the earth, returning it to the womb from where the dead could be reborn in the afterlife.

The Egyptians believed each person was made up of five

TUTANKHAMUN

essential elements; the ka, the ba, the akh, the name and the
shadow. The first three of these do not easily correspond to
any concepts of the person held in the modern, western
world, which makes them difficult to translate. The ka, something like the life force, and the ba, the personality or spirit,
of an individual became separated at death, when the ka left
the body. For a dead person to progress on his or her journey
into the afterlife, the ka and ba had to be reunited to form the
akh, the form which the dead would take for eternity. The
name and shadow were also held to be vital parts of a
complete person and, for the dead to live on in the afterlife,
both had to be preserved through inscriptions and statues.
This was why the pharaohs of the 18th Dynasty built so many
monuments to themselves and inscribed their names on so
many occasions. It also explains why these monuments were
destroyed and the names erased by later pharaohs who
wanted to obliterate the memory of a predecessor. By doing
so, they were preventing the predecessor from living on in
the afterlife and, in effect, killing him for a second time.

The body of a dead person was important because it was
the place to which the ka returned when it was reunited with
the ba, so it had to be preserved for this process to occur.
Mummification is thought to have been a development arising
out of the natural preservation that occurred to bodies when
they were buried in the arid conditions of the Western
Desert. Desiccation obviously would not occur naturally
when a body was buried in a tomb, so it had to be done arti-
ficially by embalming. The first part of the process involved
the removal of the internal organs and viscera, which were
embalmed themselves and placed in canopic jars in the tomb.
At least in the case of the pharaohs, the brain was removed as

well. Bags of natron, a naturally occurring mineral salt, were placed in the body cavity and the body was covered with more natron. This was left for a period of 40 days, during which time the natron drew the moisture out of the body. The cavity was cleaned with ointments and filled with more bags of fresh natron and resin-soaked cloth so that it maintained its shape.

The embalming process resulted in the darkening of the body's skin and the resin also blackened over time. It was this dark colour which led to the embalmed bodies being called mummies, a corruption of the Arabic word for bitumen, *mummiya*, although, in fact, this substance was very rarely used in mummification. The final procedure involved wrapping the body in long strips of linen, which were usually made from old clothes. During the wrapping, various amulets, or charms in the form of jewellery, were placed in specific places within the linen strips. The Book of the Dead includes passages giving instructions where particular amulets should be placed to give protection to the mummy.

As well as preserving the body for the afterlife, the Egyptians believed the dead had to be provisioned for the journey through the underworld, so food and drink were included in the tomb. Everything else thought to be needed was also supplied: clothes, furniture, weapons, chariots and a wide variety of other items. If the necessary piece of equipment was too big to be put in the tomb itself, a model was included instead. Tutankhamun, for example, had been provided with 35 model boats in a variety of designs, from ceremonial solar barques, intended to be used by the pharaoh in his journey through the afterlife, to more practical designs, ranging from small, single-person reed boats up to river-going sailing ships. More than 400 shabtis were also found in the tomb. These were figurines who, according to Egyptian belief, would work for the pharaoh in the afterlife, doing the agricultural and building labour he would require, and they were equipped with a variety of implements and tools for these purposes.

The 18th Dynasty pharaohs began to use tombs cut into the rock on the side of a wadi in the Theban Hills, now known as the Valley of the Kings, under the pyramid-shaped hill known as al-Qurn. The resemblance of this hill to the primordial mound of the Egyptian creation myths, also thought to have influenced the building of the pyramids during the Old Kingdom, could have been one reason for the choice of this particular wadi. A more practical reason was its isolated position, making the tombs easier to protect against robbers.

The position of the royal tombs in the Valley of the Kings did not allow for the building of temples, where the names of pharaohs were kept alive in rituals conducted by family members and priests. These had to be built separately and were usually situated on the western bank of the Nile just above the level of the flood. Well-known examples include the mortuary temples of Hatshepsut at Deir el Bahri and of Ramesses III, the 19th Dynasty pharaoh, at Medinet Habu. Nothing remains of Tutankhamun's mortuary temple, although it is thought to have been at Medinet Habu, where two colossal statues originally from his temple were reused in Ay's temple, itself usurped by Horemheb.

The Tomb and the Funeral

Tutankhamun's tomb, as already discussed, was relatively small for the burial of a pharaoh and quite simple in design. It was cut into the limestone bedrock at the bottom of the Valley of the Kings and was entered by descending a flight of 16 steps, which led down to a doorway and on into a downward sloping passageway. The tomb itself was composed of four chambers, described by Howard Carter as the antechamber, the annex, the burial chamber and the treasury. The walls of all these chambers, with the exception of the burial chamber, were left unplastered. Chisel marks left by the masons who cut out the tomb can still be seen today, together with the red marks they made on walls while they were working. Howard Carter found limestone chippings on the floor on the antechamber, indicating that the masons either did not have the time or the inclination to clear the tomb properly before Tutankhamun's funeral began.

The passageway opened into the antechamber, where three ritual couches were placed, each designed to show the features of a god or goddess in the forms of a lion, a bull and a hippopotamus. Other items of furniture, chests and the parts of chariots were also placed in this room, and they appear to have been scattered by robbers shortly after the funeral. The annex, a smaller chamber leading off from the antechamber, had also been left in disarray by the robbers, but appears to have been intended originally as a storeroom for food and wine.

The burial chamber, containing Tutankhamun's sarcophagus, was situated in an unusual position if Tutankhamun's tomb is compared to the tombs of other 18th Dynasty pharaohs. On entering the antechamber from the passageway, the burial chamber would normally be found directly to the front but, in Tutankhamun's tomb, it was off to the right. The final room was the treasury, which was entered through a doorway in the burial chamber. A gilded wooden shrine was placed in this doorway and, on top of this, a life-sized image of the jackal god Anubis rested, with its long tail almost reaching down to the ground and its huge ears pricked. Presumably Anubis had been placed there to protect the canopic shrine within, which contained four jars where the embalmed viscera removed from Tutankhamun's body during mummification were stored.

The body was mummified very much in the manner detailed in the previous section. Tutankhamun's arms were crossed in front of him, in the pose typical of royal mummies, and he was holding the flail and crook, symbols of his position as pharaoh. Before the body was wrapped in linen bandages, Tutankhamun's head had been shaved and his body anointed with oils. A beaded cap, decorated, rather surprisingly, with a cartouche containing the Aten, was placed on his head. It is the only part of the funeral regalia to remain in place to this day. Howard Carter failed to remove it after he had unwrapped the mummy because it was too firmly stuck to Tutankhamun's head. A pair of golden sandals was placed on his feet and the body adorned with a variety of amulets, including necklaces, one bearing a scarab inscribed with a spell from the Book of the Dead, and bracelets of gold inlaid with semi-precious stones. Two daggers were also placed with the body, one made of gold and the other of iron, a rare and prestigious metal in Egypt at the time and one only used for ceremonial objects. The body was then wrapped and many more protective amulets and others charms were placed within the bandages, in accordance with the spells set out in the Book of the Dead.

Once the mummy had been prepared, the funeral itself

could take place. The east wall of the burial chamber in the tomb was painted with a scene from the funeral procession. Tutankhamun's mummified body, with his name written in hieroglyphs above it, is shown lying on a bed, surrounded by an elaborate shrine. It sits on a boat, which is itself resting on a sledge, and the whole assemblage is being pulled along by 12 important members of Tutankhamun's court. They are all wearing white headbands, showing they are in mourning, and two of them have shaven heads. These are Tutankhamun's viziers, who are not identified, but could be Pentu and Usermont, the only two viziers whose names are known to us. The text above them reads 'Osiris, Lord of the Two Lands, Nebkhepepure [Tutankhamun's throne name] to the west. They say in one voice, Nebkhepepure come in peace, God, protector of the land.' The sledge is being symbolically dragged towards the west, where the sun goes down into the underworld, the realm of Osiris.

The paintings on the north wall show three separate scenes. In the first, Tutankhamun's mummy, which has taken on the form of Osiris, is facing Ay, dressed in the leopard skin of a sem priest, the priest who officiates at funerals, and wearing the blue crown of Egypt. In Egyptian mythology, Horus took charge of the burial of his father Osiris and, in showing Ay performing these duties, the painting is proclaiming him as Tutankhamun's son and heir. Cartouches bearing the names of the dead pharaoh and the succeeding pharaoh have been placed together over their images, reinforcing the message. Ay is conducting the Opening of the Mouth Ceremony, a long and elaborate funeral ritual carried out by the heir to the throne, which symbolically revived the mummy, allowing it to breathe and making it ready for the reunion of its ka and ba. It would have been the last ritual performed before Tutankhamun's mummy was interred in its nest of coffins and placed in the sarcophagus.

In the second scene on the north wall, Tutankhamun is being welcomed into the afterlife by Nut, the mother of Osiris and the goddess who renewed the sun each morning. The final scene shows Tutankhamun's mummy, closely followed by his ka, which is just about to be reunited with his ba, being embraced by Osiris, who will lead him into the afterlife.

On the other side of the burial chamber, on the south wall where the doorway is situated, is a companion piece showing Tutankhamun being welcomed into the afterlife by the goddess Hathor, the daughter of Ra, who was regarded as the divine mother of the pharaohs and, in mythology, received the setting sun in the evening and protected it until the morning. She is holding up to his nose an ankh symbol, which is T-shaped with a loop at the top and denoted life. Anubis, the jackal-headed god of embalming, stands behind Tutankhamun with his hand on the pharaoh's shoulder. The rest of the decoration on the south wall was extensively damaged when Howard Carter and his workmen were removing the shrines from the tomb. It showed Isis, another mother figure to the pharaoh, offering Tutankhamun a drink of water, perhaps as a symbol of the restoration of his power.

The paintings on the west wall appear at first sight to be the strangest of all the wall decorations. On the lower part of the wall there are 12 boxes, each of which contains the squatting figure of a baboon. Above the baboons a scarab beetle, a representation of the sun god Khepri who was associated with resurrection, is shown in a boat, often described as a solar barque. The scarab is flanked by two images of Osiris and, next to the barque, there are five more deities, including Maat and Horus. This is the culmination of the artistic scheme of the burial chamber. It is an illustration of one part of the Book of Amduat, a funerary text reserved for royalty, which guides the pharaoh to the afterlife. It tells the story of Ra's journey through the underworld during the 12 hours of night, from the sunset in the west to the sunrise at dawn, the same journey the dead pharaoh will take if he follows the instructions in the book. Baboons were considered sacred animals by the Egyptians, who thought of them as the embodiments of the dead. This probably developed from their observations of the habitual behaviour of troops of baboons, who will sit together in the characteristic squatting position shown in the paintings to watch the sun rise and set. There are twelve of them to indicate the 12 hours of night. They are watching the rebirth of the sun in the morning and, as the pharaoh travels with the sun, they are also watching Tutankhamun being reborn.

After the Opening of the Mouth Ceremony, the mummy was ready to be interred in the sarcophagus already in place in the burial chamber. The golden funeral mask, undoubtedly one of the most famous artefacts now surviving from the ancient world, was placed over the mummy's head. It is a supreme example of the artistry and skill of Egyptian craftsmen and shows an idealised portrait of Tutankhamun in full regal regalia. It was made from two sheets of solid gold, beaten together to form a sheet of almost exactly even thickness, except for a small spot on the left cheek, and inlaid with semi-precious stones, such as lapis lazuli and turquoise, together with faience and coloured glass. The blue strips of the pharaoh's nemes headdress stand out from the gold, as do the outline of the eyes, which are themselves made from quartz and obsidian. A golden uraeus of a rearing cobra, the goddess Wadjet of Lower Egypt, and the vulture goddess Nekhbet of Upper Egypt are positioned on the front of the headdress, on the pharaoh's forehead. A curled and braided false beard, a symbol of the divinity of the pharaohs, hangs down from the chin of the mask and is made from gold with inlaid faience to suggest the braiding. A broad collar hangs around the neck and shoulders and this is also made of gold, inlaid with rows of more semi-precious stones and coloured glass. The text of a spell from the Book of the Dead has been engraved on the back of the mask, providing Tutankhamun with yet more protection for his journey through the underworld.

The mummy was further adorned with a pair of burnished gold hands, fixed on to the outer linen wrapping and holding the pharaoh's crook and flail. Four gold bands encircled the mummy laterally and one, ending in a bird representing the ba, vertically. These bore the name Ankhkhepure, identifying them as having been made initially for a different mummy, possibly Smenkhare. The original owner appears to have had a different body shape to Tutankhamun as the bands had to be modified to fit his mummy.

The fully prepared and adorned mummy was then placed in the nest of three coffins within the sarcophagus. All three coffins were designed to show an image of the pharaoh, although, as already discussed, the second coffin was facially very different from the other two. The inner coffin was made from 240 lbs (110kg) of solid gold and the other two were of gilded wood. All had been inlaid in a similar way to the mask.

The outer coffin was slightly too big to fit into the sarcophagus and had been quickly modified by having a small piece roughly sawn off it at the bottom. The final parts of the burial assemblage were four gilded wooden shrines, which were erected around the sarcophagus after it had been sealed. Each was elaborately decorated with gods and goddesses and funerary text and they all had doors facing to the east. This appears to have been a last minute decision. The shrines seem to have been originally designed with the doors to the west and to have been reorganised at the last moment. The final outer shrine almost completely filled the burial chamber. Various items were left in the small gap between this shrine and the burial chamber wall, including eleven wooden paddles, presumably placed there so that Tutankhamun's solar barque could be rowed on its journey into the afterlife.

A funeral banquet would no doubt have been held, either before the Opening of the Mouth Ceremony or after the mummy had been sealed in the sarcophagus. This would probably have taken place in a tent outside the tomb and the remnants of the feast ceremonially buried. A pit on the other side of the wadi from the tomb, classified as KV54, was found in 1907 and it contained a number of large storage jars with material in them associated with Tutankhamun's funeral. Pottery dishes and the remains of food were found, thought to be from the banquet, and there were other items, such as bags of natron, which had been used during the mummification process. Research has shown that, in all probability, the jars had originally been placed in the entrance passageway of the tomb itself and were removed after it had been entered by robbers. The passageway was then filled with rubble in an attempt to prevent further robberies. The material removed from the tomb was given a separate burial in the pit, which appears to have been the entrance shaft for an unfinished and abandoned tomb.

After the funeral, and once all the grave goods were in place, the doorways into the burial chamber, antechamber and annex were filled with stone, plastered over and stamped with seals. The tomb was now complete and the entrance doorway at the bottom of the steps into the tomb was finally blocked and sealed. The tomb was entered on at least two occasions by robbers, probably not long after it was first sealed. After the robberies, the tomb was tidied up in a fairly perfunctory manner and the doors resealed. It was these seal impressions that would identify the tomb as belonging to Tutankhamun when Howard Carter uncovered them in 1922, some 3,300 years after they had been made.

The End of the Line

The Zannanza Affair

Included in the Amarna Letters cache is a small amount of correspondence between the Hittite king Suppiluliuma I and Akhenaten, in which Suppiluliuma I expresses his wish for the continuation of good relations between the two empires, as had been the case during the reign of Amenhotep III. Although the chronology of events is difficult to follow, this does not appear to have been what happened. The Hittites and Egyptians became involved in a long-running border war, both apparently attempting to maintain their influence with those states in the disputed territory between the empires in northern Syria.

At some stage, relations between the two were further soured by a diplomatic incident arising from a letter written by the wife of an Egyptian king to Suppiluliuma I which resulted in the death of one of his sons. Although this was not the only cause of the ongoing animosity between the Hittites and Egypt, which was ultimately about control of territory, it would lead to an escalation of the war between them. The struggle for power would continue for more than a hundred years, until a peace accord was reached between the Egyptian pharaoh Ramesses II and the Hittite king Mutwalli II after the inconclusive Battle of Kadesh, fought in 1274 BC near the Orontes River in Syria and thought to have been the largest chariot battle ever fought.

The Zannanza Affair, named after the son of Suppiluliuma I who was killed, came to light after a huge archive of documents was discovered in archaeological excavations of the Hittite capital of Hattusha, near the modern village of Bogazkale in central Anatolia. The archive was not unlike the Amarna Letters, but it was on a much larger scale. Something like 30,000 clay tablets have been found and they include documents covering the official business of the king, correspondence, religious texts, literature and legal documents. One of the documents found was the peace treaty between the Hittites and Egyptians after the Battle of Kadesh, a copy of which is displayed in the United Nations Building in New York.

Another set of tablets contain the writings of Mursili II, one of Suppiluliuma I's younger sons who would ascend to the throne after the deaths of his father and his older brother Arnuwanda II, both of whom are thought to have died from an outbreak of the plague spread to the Hittite Empire from Egyptian prisoners of war. Mursili II wrote about the achievements of his father, the set of tablets generally being referred to under the title The Deeds of Suppiluliuma, and in one section he appeared to quote from the correspondence between Suppiluliuma I and an Egyptian woman given the title 'Dakhamunza' which, since the Egyptians did not have a specific word for 'queen', is usually translated as 'the King's Wife'. Mursili II wrote:

> While my father was in the country of Karkemish (in North Syria), he sent Luppaki and Turhunda-Zalma into

the country of Amqa (further south from Karkemish). They attacked Amqa and brought prisoners, and cattle and sheep back to my father. When the people of Egypt heard of the attack on Amqa, they were afraid. Their lord Nibkhururiya had recently died and the queen of Egypt, who was Dakhamunza, sent an ambassador to my father with a message saying 'My husband is dead and I have no son. It is said you have many sons. If you send one of your sons to me, he would become my husband. I will never take a servant of mine as a husband. I am afraid'.

Mursili named the Egyptian pharaoh who had recently died as Nibkhururiya. Unfortunately it is not possible to be absolutely certain who he is talking about, although the most likely candidate is Tutankhamun, who would probably have been known to the Hittites by his throne name of Nebkheperure. It does not take a great leap of the imagination to recognise the similarities between the two names, particularly when one considers the level of translation and transliteration that both have gone through. Nibkhururiya is a transliteration of the Hittite cuneiform script into the Roman script, while the Hittites themselves arrived at the name from transliterations of Egyptian hieroglyphs into Akkadian, the Babylonian language of diplomacy, which had then to be translated into Hittite. With each stage the possibility of errors creeping in increases, so, considering the level of abstraction involved, the names are surprisingly similar. The identification of Tutankhamun with this episode can only be tentative but, if it is him, then Dakhamunza, the writer of the letter, must be his widow Ankhesenamun.

The account given by Mursili continued with his father

calling a meeting of his council to discuss the contents of the letter. Suppiluliuma addressed the council, saying he had never heard of such a thing before. At the time alliances between states were regularly sealed by a daughter from one royal household being sent to another to become the king's wife, but this was a request for a son, who would become the ruler of Egypt, thereby uniting the two empires into what would now be called a superpower. Suppiluliuma was suspicious and decided to send an ambassador to Egypt to find out if the offer was genuine or if it was some sort of Egyptian trick. Mursili goes on with the account:

> The queen of Egypt wrote back to my father in a letter saying, 'Why did you think I tried to deceive you? If I had a son, would I have brought shame on myself and my country by writing to you in a foreign land? But you have told me you do not believe me. My husband has died and I do not have a son. I will never take a servant of mine and make him my husband. I have written to no other country, only to you. They say you have many sons. Give one of them to me and he will be my husband. In Egypt he will be king.' My father was a generous man so he decided to grant the woman's request to send her one of his sons.

The circumstances in which the King's Wife found herself certainly fitted those of Ankhesenamun after Tutankhamun's death. She must have been in a precarious position as the royal widow. Whoever married her could legitimately claim the right to become the next pharaoh, but there was nobody left from the royal bloodline. Egyptian royal women were bound by convention only to marry somebody of similar status to themselves, so, if the letter writer was really Ankhesenamun, perhaps she would have looked to the royal family of the Hittites for a suitable partner.

Much of the rest of the account given by Mursili is frag-mentary, but, taken together with an exchange of letters between Suppiluliuma and an Egyptian pharaoh (the pharaoh, frustratingly, is not named), it is possible to reconstruct the enfolding events. The Hittite king sent one of his sons, Zannanza, to Egypt, but he did not arrive, having died some-where along the way. Suppiluliuma wrote to Egypt to find out what had happened to his son and got a reply from the new pharaoh, possibly Ay, bluntly telling him that his son was dead. The author of the letter went on to say that he was now the ruler of Egypt, but denied having had anything to do with Zannanza's death. Suppiluliuma did not accept the new pharaoh's account and initiated an attack on the Egyptian territory in what is now known as the Beqaa Valley in eastern Lebanon.

The timescale for these events, as provided by Mursili and the letters, makes clear that the pharaoh died before Suppiluliuma had retired to his capital for the winter and that the correspondence between the two rulers occurred the following spring, by which time the new pharaoh had assumed power in Egypt. This fits in the events of Tutankhamun's death and the succession of Ay, assuming there was a longer gap between Tutankhamun's death and his funeral than the traditional 70-day period taken for the mummification of his body. The way in which Mursili discusses the death of the pharaoh he calls Nibkhururiya suggests that, if this is Tutankhamun, then he did not die in battle against the Hittites, who were Egypt's main opponents at the time. If the Hittites had been responsible for the death of a pharaoh, Mursili would surely have made much more of it than he did when recounting the events.

The evidence linking this episode to the period immediately following Tutankhamun's death is entirely circumstantial and, just because the account given by Mursili corresponds with the little we know of this period, it does not necessarily follow that it is exactly what happened. It will take the discovery of more convincing evidence than is currently available to be able to say for certain that Ankhesenamun was prepared to marry a Hittite prince rather than suffer the ignominy of marrying a commoner from her own court. In any event, the death of Zannanza, by whatever means it occurred, put an end to the plans and led to a period of intense fighting between the Hittites and Egypt.

Political Manoeuvring

Whether the Zannanza affair had any direct bearing on the events occurring after Tutankhamun's death or not, he was certainly the last pharaoh in the Thutsomid line that began with Thutmose I in about 1504 BC, almost 175 years before. His death, leaving no male heir, created a power vacuum at the top of the Egyptian hierarchy which, it seems, should have been filled by Horemheb. He appears to have been Tutankhamun's designated heir, bearing the titles of Crown Prince and Deputy of the Lord of the Two Lands but, for some unknown reason, he did not succeed to the throne.

As has been shown in the previous chapter, the duties of preparing and then conducting Tutankhamun's funeral were performed by Ay, duties that could be performed by the heir to the throne alone. The circumstances of Ay's rise to power are unclear and there are a number of theories to explain why he succeeded Tutankhamun in place of Horemheb. One of these theories suggests that Horemheb was not part of Tutankhamun's funeral preparations because he was in northern Syria as commander-in-chief of the Egyptian army campaigning against the Hittites. There certainly appears to have been an Egyptian confrontation with the Hittites over Amqa in the Lebanon which occurred at this time and, if this was the case, it would have represented an incursion by the Hittites deep into Egyptian-controlled territory. It would be reasonable to suppose that Horemheb would have commanded the response to this crisis.

Another theory has Ay succeeding Tutankhamun because he was a diplomat rather than a military leader. According to an inscription in the tomb constructed for him in Saqqara while he was a senior member of Tutankhamun's court, Horemheb was well known to the Hittites, presumably through facing them in battle. It is possible that he did not succeed Tutankhamun because the Egyptians did not want to antagonise the Hittites, who were apparently gaining the upper hand in Syria at the time, by declaring a man with a reputation as a military leader as pharaoh. A continuation of this theory has Ay and Horemheb reaching an understanding whereby the older man, Ay, ascends to the throne first, to be succeeded by the younger man on his death. The problem with this theory is that, after Ay's death, Horemheb attempted to remove Ay's name from all the monuments he erected during his reign and desecrated Ay's tomb immediately after his death. These actions do not seem to be those of a man who had reached an agreement with Ay over the succession.

The exact circumstances of the succession may be open to conjecture but there can be no doubt that Ay, by some means or another, ascended to the throne after Tutankhamun. Prior to becoming pharaoh, he had been a prominent figure in the royal court for more than 30 years, going back to the reign of Amenhotep III. He must have acquired a wealth of experience in the procedures and intrigues of the administration. It is not hard to imagine him outmanoeuvring Horemheb, a much younger man who was probably more familiar with military matters than the workings of the court.

Ay's parentage is not known, but he is thought to have been originally from the town of Akhmin in Upper Egypt. After he became pharaoh, he erected a temple there to the local god Min, an act which certainly suggests strong ties to the area. Yuya and Tuyu, the parents of Amenhotep III's Great Royal Wife Tiye, were also from Akhmin and, although no evidence exists to confirm a family relationship between them, such a link would explain Ay's rise to a prominent position in the royal court. Another theory maintains that Ay and his wife Tey were the parents of Nefertiti but, since her origins are completely obscure, it is not possible to verify this claim. Considering the prevalence of incestuous relationships within the Egyptian royal family, it is not beyond the realms of possibility for Ay to have had all of these family relationships at the same time, which would make him both Nefertiti's father and her uncle-in-law.

Whatever Ay's family relations were, he was not of royal blood and, in the strictly hierarchical royal court, this meant he should not have been a legitimate heir to the throne. A marriage to Tutankhamun's widow Ankhesenamun would certainly have improved his claim, although, if Ay was

Nefertiti's father, he would also be Ankhesenamun's grandfather. A blue faience ring, now in the Altes Museum in
Berlin, has been inscribed with two cartouches containing the
names of Ay and Ankhesenamun, which have been placed next
to each other. This is the only extant evidence to signify a
marriage between the two of them and it is also the last
known reference to Ankhesenamun after Tutankhamun's
death. There is no mention of her in Ay's tomb, KV23, in the
Valley of the Kings which, although extensively damaged after
his death, does include two wall paintings of his Great Royal
Wife Tey. The tomb of Ankhesenamun, assuming she had one,
has not been found but, should it be discovered, it may well
shed some light on the events of the succession.

Ay must have been an old man by the time he gained the
throne, probably in his mid-60s. He reigned from 1327 BC to
1323 BC, dying at some point in his fourth regnal year, but
very little information on the events of this period has
survived. A statue of the high-level military officer Nakhtmin
in the Egyptian Museum in Cairo, dating to Ay's reign, carries
an inscription to say that he is the King's Son. This has been
taken to mean that Nakhtmin was Ay's designated heir, rather
than Horemheb. It does not necessarily imply that Nakhtmin
was actually Ay's son, although his name contains a reference
to the god Min, suggesting he came from the same town as Ay.
Not a great deal is known about Nakhtmin, although five
shabti figures bearing inscriptions to say they were donated by
him were found in Tutankhamun's tomb, indicating he was a
close associate of the pharaoh. It is not known if he died
before Ay or if Horemheb managed to push him aside after
Ay's death, but, for whatever reason, he did not succeed to
the throne.

Horemheb and a New Dynasty

The family background of Horemheb is obscure. He probably came from Herakleopolis, the religious centre of the god Horus, and was married twice, first to a woman called Amenia, who appears to have died before he became pharaoh, and then to Mutnedjmet. Speculation concerning the identity of this second wife has suggested she could have been Nefertiti's sister but, as the name Mutnedjmet was not particularly rare at the time, it is impossible to know for certain. It seems unlikely Horemheb would have married Nefertiti's sister to give legitimacy to his claim to the throne because this would have associated him with Akhenaten and the Amarna Period and his subsequent actions make it improbable that he would have wanted this. On his Coronation Stele, now in the Egyptian Museum in Turin, Horemheb makes no claim to be descended from any previous pharaoh but says instead that he was chosen by the oracle of Horus at Herakleopolis, giving him a divine right to rule. The Coronation Stele also carries details of his former position as regent during Tutankhamun's reign, perhaps a justification for him gaining the throne instead of Ay's chosen successor Nakhtmin.

Horemheb may have had to wait for his chance to become pharaoh but, once he had achieved his ambition, he appears to have wasted little time in stamping his authority on the country. He set about erasing the memories of his immediate predecessors by demolishing the monuments they built and removing their names from inscriptions. The entire royal line connected to Akhenaten, including Smenkhare and Tutankhamun, was targeted but he seems to have held a particular grudge against Ay. Although not proven beyond

doubt, it is highly likely that he was responsible for the dese-
cration of Ay's tomb. Every reference to Ay was obliterated
and representations of Ay's face have been chipped out of wall
paintings. When the tomb was first discovered by Giovanni
Belzoni in 1816, Ay's sarcophagus had been smashed into
numerous pieces, the amount of damage done being much
greater than would be expected as a result of the actions of
tomb robbers. In an act that would ensure Ay's name did not
live on, Horemheb also usurped his mortuary temple at
Medinet Habu, replacing the inscriptions concerning Ay with
his own.

If Horemheb was taking revenge on Ay, he does not appear
to have felt so strongly towards Tutankhamun. Although he
removed Tutankhamun's name wherever he found it, the
tomb was not touched. Akhenaten was not so lucky. The
demolition of the city of Amarna continued throughout
Horemheb's reign and the only people living there at this time
appear to have been those carrying out the work of destruction. The temple built by Akhenaten at Karnak was also
demolished and the rubble used again in the building of the
Ninth and Tenth Pylon of the Precinct of Amun. Reusing
blocks bearing inscriptions relating to Akhenaten has actually
had the effect of preserving some of them, so Horemheb's
attempts to obliterate the memory of Akhenaten have, on this
occasion, not been entirely successful. According to some
scholars, Horemheb was also responsible for starting the
construction of the Great Hypostyle Hall in the same
precinct, the huge stone columns of which are one of the
most recognisable monuments in Egypt. The more conventional view is that the hall was actually begun during the reign
of Sety I and continued under Ramesses II.

The rejection of Akhenaten's reforms can be seen to have started during the reign of Tutankhamun, as shown in the text of the Restoration Stele, but it reached its high point under Horemheb. According to an inscription erected on a stele in front of the Tenth Pylon at Karnak, known as the Great Edict, Horemheb also intended to restore order and the rule of law to the country and put a stop to the corrupt practices he claimed were rampant under the previous administrations. The text of the Great Edict sets out a number of reforms and lists punishments that will apply to government officials, particularly to tax collectors and the army, should they continue to break the law.

The length of Horemheb's reign is far from certain, and the task of calculating it accurately is not helped by the tendency at the time, no doubt encouraged by Horemheb himself, to count the number of years of his rule as if it started with the death of Amenhotep III, and the intervening pharaohs had not existed at all. Little evidence remains to confirm he continued to rule after his thirteenth regnal year, except for graffiti found on a statue at his mortuary temple, which states it was written during the twenty-seventh year of his reign. A later text, known as the Inscription of Mes, dating from the reign of Ramesses II, tends to confirm the graffiti. It concerns a protracted legal case between members of a family which has been interpreted as beginning during Horemheb's twenty-seventh year.

The apparently unfinished state of his tomb in the Valley of the Kings, KV57, has been put forward as evidence that he could not have ruled for such a long period, although it is not unprecedented for building work on a tomb to continue throughout the pharaoh's life. Horemheb's second wife Mutnedjmet died in the thirteenth year of his reign and was buried in the tomb at Saqqara, prepared for him before he became pharaoh, where his first wife had also been buried. A mummy found in the tomb had a still-born child with it, leading to the conclusion that Mutnedjmet died in childbirth, perhaps, as she was more than 40 years old, in a late attempt to provide Horemheb with an heir. If he had any other children, none of them survived him. During the later part of his reign, he relied heavily on a fellow military officer called Paramessu, who held a number of posts in the army and civil administration, including vizier and High Priest of Amun. Horemheb was in the habit of appointing former army officers to the Priesthood of Amun, perhaps as a means of rewarding people he had commanded when he was commander-in-chief of the army himself and also as a means of keeping control of the priesthood.

One of Paramessu's lesser titles was Commander of Site, an important fortress on the eastern frontier of Egypt. The appointment of the person who was, in effect, Horemheb's right-hand man to this post is an indication of the continuing problems Egypt was having in Syria and Palestine. There is some suggestion in the Hittite archives in Hattusha of an accommodation having been reached between them and Horemheb but, if this was the case, peace appears to have been fragmentary. Either an uneasy calm or open warfare between the two powers seems to have been the more usual state of affairs.

Horemheb died without an heir in about 1295 BC and was succeed by Paramessu, who, on becoming pharaoh, took the name usually written in English as Ramesses, meaning 'Born of Ra'. He was the third successive pharaoh who was not of royal blood and used the same kind of justification as

Horemheb had to legitimise his rule, although Ramesses claimed to have been chosen by the god Seth, suggesting he was from the former Hyksos capital of Avaris, where Seth was the principal local deity.

One of Horemheb's reasons for choosing Ramesses as his successor could have been because he already had a son who could succeed him and, more than likely, a grandson as well to continue the line. The dynasty founded by Ramesses, the 19th Dynasty, continued with his son Sety I and he was followed by Ramesses II, or Ramesses the Great as he is sometimes known, now regarded as the most powerful of all the pharaohs. Ramesses the Great ruled for 66 years, during which time he is reputed to have fathered more than 100 children. He died in about 1279 BC, when he was more than 90 years old.

The Pharaonic Period is conventionally said to have lasted for almost another 1,000 years after the death of Ramesses II, although this does not take into account a number of periods of Persian rule. In 332 BC Alexander the Great conquered Egypt, putting an end to the rule of the pharaohs and bringing in the Ptolemaic Period, which would itself end in 30 BC with the machinations of Cleopatra and Mark Antony and the absorption of Egypt into the Roman Empire after the Battle of Actium.

The Discovery of the Tomb

Egyptology

In the eighteenth century, orientalism, an interest in all things to do with the East, became fashionable in the high society of Western Europe. The expansion of European empires through India and the Far East brought increased contact between East and West and this led to a certain amount of academic interest in Eastern cultures, mainly directed towards describing what was considered mysterious and exotic rather than towards serious attempts to understand the Orient, as everywhere beyond Greece was called at the time. The modern study of Egyptology is said to have begun either in 1798, with Napoleon's expedition to Egypt, or, alternatively, in 1822, when Jean-François Champollion announced that he had deciphered the hieroglyphic inscription on the Rosetta Stone in the British Museum. This was certainly the start of a much greater understanding of the Pharaonic Period in Egypt, but western academics had been aware of Ancient Egypt for many years before this and Arab scholars, largely unknown and unrecognised in the West, had been working in Egypt for many centuries. They had been studying the monuments and texts of Ancient Egypt since the Arab invasion of the country in AD 639 and there is evidence that they had an understanding of the meaning of hieroglyphs as early as the ninth century AD.

Europe, particularly Britain and France, had more material interests in Egypt than purely academic ones. Competing colonial ambitions between the two countries were evident in many parts of the world and the commercial advantages of a canal through Egypt, connecting the Mediterranean Sea and the Red Sea, were obvious to both. Opening up a much shorter sea route to the Far East and India than the hazardous voyage around the Cape of Good Hope was potentially a financial goldmine. The French initially secured the concession to build the Suez canal from the Egyptian Government, then a largely autonomous province of the Ottoman Empire, in 1858. It opened in 1869 and was immediately hugely profitable. Due to a financial crisis in their country, the Egyptians sold their stake in the canal to Britain in the 1870s. From then on, Britain and France jointly administered the canal and, in all but name, ran the country as well. Britain invaded Egypt in 1882, claiming it did so to protect its interest in the canal from the growing nationalist movement within the country and, although Egypt nominally remained a part of the Ottoman Empire until the outbreak of the First World War, it was effectively a British colony.

At about this time Egyptology, and archaeology in general, was undergoing its own revolution. From being solely the pastime of wealthy collectors of antiquities or of explorers and adventurers like the colourful Giovanni Belzoni, who supplied the trade in Egyptian artefacts, it was slowly becoming an academic discipline. Pioneers of archaeology were introducing much more rigorous and systematic techniques into the study of prehistory and huge finds were being made. Heinrich Schliemann was discovering extraordinary artefacts in Mycenae and Troy and Sir Arthur Evans was uncovering evidence of the Minoan civilisation at Knossos in Crete. It was a golden age of archaeology, although the interpretation of some of the finds often had more to do with wish fulfilment than an examination of the actual evidence.

One of the first to apply the new techniques of excavation to Egypt was Sir Flinders Petrie who began working in the country in 1880. By 1892, Petrie was leading an excavation in Amarna and a young man called Howard Carter, who had arrived in Egypt the year before to work as an archaeological draughtsman, came under the tutelage of the great man. Petrie was distinctly unimpressed by the 18-year-old Carter, saying he could not foresee a future for the young man in Egyptology. Carter, even at such a young age, was not a man to be easily put off and would continue working in Egypt over the next 40 years, going on to make the most famous archaeological discovery of all.

Howard Carter and Lord Carnarvon

With little formal education of any sort, let alone in a relevant discipline, Howard Carter was not the most obvious candidate to become one of the best-known archaeologists of his day. He was frequently unwell as a child and remained at the family home in the village of Swaffham in Norfolk rather than going to school. His father was an accomplished artist and illustrator and, no doubt, encouraged his son to follow suit. Carter was introduced to Egyptology by Lady Amherst, who lived nearby in Norfolk and was married to a well-known collector of antiquities. She noticed his artistic talent and growing interest in Egypt and mentioned him to the archaeologist Percy Newberry, who was employed by the Egypt Exploration Society and was involved in the excavation of the Middle Kingdom tombs at Beni Hasan. In those days aristocratic patronage was at least as important as academic qualifications and Newberry offered the 17-year-old Carter a job making copies of the wall paintings in the Beni Hasan tombs.

Carter would spend the next eight years learning about the techniques of archaeology from some of the best-known names in the business. He progressed from making drawings to working on excavations himself. If he had not overly impressed Sir Flinders Petrie, others in the field paid more attention. He was methodical and hard working and possessed the essential qualities of doggedness and persever-ance, even if these same qualities would occasionally irritate many of the people who worked with him. By 1900, Carter had been noticed by Gaston Maspero, a French archaeologist who was then the head of the Egyptian Antiquities Service, the department of the Government charged with the admin-istration of archaeological excavations and the protection of ancient monuments which would, after Egyptian independ-ence in 1956, become the Supreme Council of Antiquities within the Egyptian Ministry of Culture. Maspero offered Carter the job of Inspector General of Monuments in Upper Egypt, a position which enabled him to become very familiar with the Valley of the Kings. He built a house near the valley and spent many hours exploring it and making extensive notes.

In 1902, the wealthy American Theodore Davis, a retired lawyer, acquired the concession to excavate the Valley of the Kings from the Antiquities Service and asked Carter to supervise the work. He made a number of important discoveries, notably the tomb of Thutmose IV. It had been looted in antiquity, when everything valuable had been removed, but still contained many of its grave goods. The wall paintings were among the best-preserved of any found in the valley and there were also graffiti, dating to the reign of Horemheb, which showed the tomb had been restored at that time. The tomb thought to have been the original resting place of Thutmose I and Hapshetsut, KV20, had been known about since Napoleon's expedition in 1798, but Carter carried out the first detailed excavation, finding Hapshetsut's sarcophagus which is now in the Egyptian Museum in Cairo.

After he had finished work on KV20 in 1904, Carter was transferred to the more prestigious job of Inspector General of Monuments in Lower Egypt, based at the Saqqara Necropolis near Memphis. Davis continued to work in the Valley of the Kings, hiring a succession of professional archaeologists in Carter's place. The move to Saqqara had unforeseen consequences for Carter. After an altercation with a group of French tourists, some of whom were, as Carter would later put it, 'much the worse for liquor', the tourists complained about him to the French Consul in Cairo. Lord Cromer, the British Consul General, did not want the incident to escalate into a diplomatic row and asked Carter to apologise. He was not a man who readily apologised, even when he was in the wrong, and certainly was not about to do so on this occasion. Despite being advised against it by everyone he knew, including Gaston Maspero who did not want to lose him, Carter resigned his position. He moved back to his house near the Valley of the Kings and began dealing in antiquities and selling the paintings he made of

Egyptian scenes to wealthy tourists staying in the Winter Palace Hotel in Luxor.

Meanwhile Theodore Davis and his team of archaeologists were making significant progress in the Valley of the Kings. Over the 12-year period of the concession they excavated more than 30 tombs. Most of the tombs had been robbed in antiquity and the ones situated lower down in the valley had been damaged by the occasional flash floods which swept through it. The most spectacular find came in 1905 with the discovery of the tomb of Yuya and Tuyu, the parents of Amenhotep III's wife Tiye, who was more than likely Tutankhamun's grandmother. The tomb was the best-preserved of all the tombs found in the Valley of the Kings up until that time. It had been robbed in antiquity but the mummies were both still intact and in remarkably good condition, as were many of the grave goods. Notable among these were the gilded coffins of Yuya and Tuyu, the throne of their granddaughter Sitamun, who was Amenhotep III's daughter, and a complete and well-preserved chariot.

Throughout the period when Davis held the concession in the valley he retained his enthusiasm for the excavations and the discoveries being made. Unfortunately this enthusiasm did not extend to recording the digs in a systematic manner or publishing detailed accounts of the tombs. Carter, known for his methodical approach, was employed by Davis to record the finds in the tomb of Yuya and Tuyu, a job which, because of the haste with which Davis wanted it done, must have been a frustrating experience for him. Being on the fringes of such a big discovery, rather than directly involved in it, must also have been difficult for Carter but, characteristically, he stuck to the task.

As the work progressed in the valley, a number of finds offered tantalising glimpses of the presence of the as-yet-undiscovered tomb of Tutankhamun. In 1906, Edward Ayrton, a respected young archaeologist who would quickly become tired of Davis' slapdash methods, found a small blue faience cup in the valley inscribed with Tutankhamun's throne name. The following year he uncovered a pit (KV54) containing a number of items connected to Tutankhamun's funeral. In January 1909, a small tomb (KV58), containing objects associated with both Tutankhamun and his successor Ay, was also found. It consisted of a corridor leading to a single, small, undecorated chamber, suggesting it had either not been finished or that it had been built for a senior figure in the royal court, who had been given the privilege of a tomb in the royal necropolis, rather than for an actual pharaoh. Davis, writing some years later and, perhaps, more in hope than expectation, declared the tomb to be the final resting place of Tutankhamun. He went on to say, 'I fear the Valley of the Kings is now exhausted,' a view shared by a number of eminent Egyptologists at the time, but not by Carter.

In 1907, Carter's fortunes took a turn for the better. He was introduced to Lord Carnarvon, a keen amateur archaeologist and collector of antiquities who had excavated in Egypt himself. It was the start of a relationship which continued for more than 15 years and the combination of Carnarvon's money and Carter's expertise would prove to be highly beneficial for both men.

George Edward Stanhope Molyneux Herbert, 5th Earl of Carnarvon, to give him his full name, was a very wealthy English aristocrat. He was one of the largest landowners in England and was connected through his wife to the enormously rich Rothschild family. In his younger years he had gained a reputation as something of a playboy, owning a string of racehorses and, in the early years of motoring, fast cars. In 1901, he was lucky to survive a high-speed accident in one of those cars and he never fully recovered his health. On the advice of his doctors he began to spend the winter months in Egypt, avoiding the cold and damp of England, and he took up the rather more sedate hobby of collecting antiquities. This gave him the excuse he needed to get out of the expatriate social life of Cairo by travelling up the Nile to stay in the Winter Palace Hotel in Luxor. By 1906, he was not content to confine his activities to collecting alone and, drawn by the excitement of the treasure hunt, he began to excavate himself.

Carnarvon's first efforts were on a modest scale. He acquired a concession from the Antiquities Service to excavate at a site not far from his hotel and hired some workmen to do the actual digging. The only find of any significance at all during his first season was a small coffin containing the mummified body of a cat but, rather than putting him off Egyptology, this fired his imagination all the more. In order to be given a more promising concession, Carnarvon was advised to show the Antiquities Service the seriousness of his intentions by sponsoring a professional archaeologist rather than carrying on in an amateur fashion himself. Gaston Maspero recommended Carter and, together, they obtained a concession to excavate at a site on the west bank of the Nile near Aswan. The knowledge and experience Carter brought to the excavation began to pay off almost immediately. Carter found the tomb of an early 18th Dynasty mayor of Thebes and another tomb containing two inscribed tablets. One of these, which became known as the Carnarvon Tablet and is now in the Egyptian Museum in Cairo, related to Kamose, the last pharaoh of the 17th Dynasty, and his struggle to reunite Upper and Lower Egypt. It contained details of Kamose's complaints that he could not travel on the Nile as far as Memphis without the permission of the Hyksos and said he was commanded by Amun to lead an attack on them in Lower Egypt.

As well as bringing his experience to the excavation work, Carter, who was equally experienced as an antiquities dealer, advised Carnarvon on the purchases he made for his collection from the thriving, and highly expensive, Egyptian antiquities market. The impressive collection of artefacts put together by Carnarvon with Carter's help would eventually be sold to the Metropolitan Museum of Art in New York, where it continues to be held.

For the next seven years Carnarvon and Carter continued to excavate during the digging seasons, which lasted until the weather became too hot in the summer months. In 1914, the 76-year-old Theodore Davis decided to give up his concession in the Valley of the Kings and Carnarvon and Carter were on hand to take it over. Davis, who died a few months later, would never know how close he came to finding Tutankhamun's tomb. Harry Burton, the last archaeologist to work with him, said after the tomb had been found that he had excavated to within six feet of the location of the discovery, but had been obliged to stop because of fears of undermining a nearby road.

Carter began excavating in the valley straight away, confident there were more discoveries to be made. Although he did not make his thoughts public at the time, his primary aim in the valley was to find Tutankhamun's tomb. The tombs of almost all the 18th Dynasty pharaohs had been found in the valley, including Tutankhamun's close predecessors, Thutmose IV and Amenhotep III, and the two pharaohs who immediately followed him, Ay and Horemheb. The only two exceptions were Akhenaten, who had initially been buried in Amarna before his mummy had been moved to an unknown location in the Valley of the Kings, and Tutankhamun. The same discoveries that had convinced Davis the valley was exhausted led Carter to the opposite conclusion. If objects with Tutankhamun's name inscribed on them and material relating to his funeral were being found in the valley, then, according to Carter's straightforward reasoning, surely the tomb was there somewhere as well.

The outbreak of the First World War put a stop to Carnarvon and Carter's work in the valley. Carter was one of the few Englishmen in Egypt who had a fluent command of Egyptian Arabic, having picked up the language through talking to the workmen he hired to do the digging in his excavations, and he spent the war years working for the British Government as a diplomatic courier and translator. Carnarvon meanwhile returned to his estates in England. During breaks in his war work, Carter went back to his house near the Valley of the Kings and began to excavate the partially cleared tomb of Amenhotep III (KV22). Carter's methodical excavation turned up numerous examples of funerary equipment overlooked by previous excavators and the finds rekindled Carnarvon's enthusiasm sufficiently for him to finance further work in the valley. By 1917, Carter was in a position to start excavating full time and the search for Tutankhamun's tomb began in earnest.

The Discovery

Beginning in the winter digging season of 1917, Carter mounted a huge effort to find Tutankhamun's tomb. One of his first decisions was to concentrate his efforts in the eastern part of the valley where Theodore Davis' archaeologists had previously made the discoveries of items relating to Tutankhamun. With record keeping from those digs almost entirely absent, Carter did not know which parts of the valley had already been investigated so he decided to excavate the entire area right down to the bedrock. It was a huge under-taking, requiring the removal of many thousands of tons of limestone rubble and sand. He hired hundreds of local workmen to do the manual labour and brought in a Decauville railway, sections of ready-made narrow gauge track, so that the waste material could be removed along it in hand pushed carts.

Despite Carter's continuing confidence, by the end of the fifth season Carnarvon was having doubts. At the time the owner of a concession to excavate in Egypt could expect to receive a share of the finds they made, with everything else going to the Egyptian Government. For all the expense Carnarvon had occurred over five years, he had very little to show for it. The only significant discovery Carter had made were a number of calcite jars which he uncovered at the entrance to the tomb of the 19th Dynasty pharaoh Merneptah. The Antiquities Service had allowed Carnarvon to keep six of them. It wasn't much to show for five years of work.

In the summer of 1922, Carnarvon asked Carter to come to Highclere Castle, his vast country house on his estate in

Berkshire, to discuss the future of the project. Carter had prepared a strategy to persuade the reluctant Carnarvon to continue financing the excavation. He showed the Earl a map of the progress he had made in the valley up until then. Only a small area directly under the entrance to the tomb of Ramesses IV (KV2) remained to be excavated. Carter had left this until last because digging there would restrict public access to the tomb above it, which, because of the extensive and well-preserved wall paintings it contained, was one of the most popular with visitors to the valley. Carter wanted one more season to finish digging in this last area and offered to pay for it himself, with Carnarvon, as owner of the concession, keeping the share of any finds that would go to the excavators. Carnarvon could not fail to be impressed by Carter's commitment and agreed to one more season which he, not Carter, would finance.

On 1 November 1922, Carter was back in the Valley of the Kings and ready to begin clearing the area under Ramesses IV's tomb. The slope from the tomb entrance down to the valley floor was mostly composed of limestone chippings, 3,000-year-old debris left by the original builders of the tomb, together with the remnants of huts they had used while the work was in progress. Even though Carter was now working under the pressure of time, he used the first three days of the excavation to draw up plans of the huts, meticulously recording their position before allowing his workmen to remove them. On the morning of the fourth day, they began to clear away the first of the huts and almost immediately found a stone step cut into the bedrock. Carter noticed a sudden hush come over the workmen, a sure sign they had found something, and, on looking himself, immediately recognised the step as being of the type cut during the 18th Dynasty for a stairway into a sunken tomb.

After excavating for five years in the valley without much success, it must have been hugely exciting to have finally found something but Carter had been working in Egypt for 30 years by that time and was not about to get too carried away. He was well aware of the possibility that the step led to an unfinished or unused tomb or that, even if it was what he was looking for, that it had been looted by robbers in antiquity, as almost all of the other tombs in the valley had been. Work continued at a feverish rate to clear the debris out of the pit into which the steps were descending.

By the following afternoon, the workmen had dug out 12 steps and were beginning to uncover the top of a doorway. It had been filled in and plastered over and, as more of it was exposed, Carter saw the seal of the Royal Necropolis, an image of a jackal, a symbol of the god Anubis, above nine figures of captives with their hands tied behind their backs. This suggested the tomb belonged to a member of an 18th Dynasty royal family but Carter was still not taking anything for granted. He could not find a seal showing a royal name stamped in the plaster and thought that it could be the tomb of a high-ranking noble or that it could have been used as a mummy cache. There were also signs of an area of the doorway being resealed, suggesting the tomb had been entered after it had been originally sealed. However, the fact that it had been sealed again indicated there was something inside to make doing this worthwhile.

Carter made a small hole in the top of the doorway and shone a torch through it onto a passageway completely filled with stones and rubble. It was getting late in the day and, with what he describes as a certain amount of reluctance, Carter instructed his workmen to refill the pit, covering the stairway up to the level of the top step. He sent a telegram to Carnarvon, who was in England at the time, saying, 'At last have made wonderful discovery in Valley; a magnificent tomb with seals intact; recovered same for your arrival; congratulations', and, before doing anything else other than securing the site and tidying up the surrounding area, he waited for Carnarvon to arrive.

If Carter felt any sense of impatience or suspense during the almost three weeks he waited for Carnarvon and his 22-year-old daughter Lady Evelyn Herbert to travel to Luxor he did not record it, saying instead that he used the time to plan what he would do if the tomb proved to be that of Tutankhamun. On the 24th November, with Carnarvon, Lady Evelyn and a number of other dignitaries in attendance, the full extent of the stairway was cleared. Carter found a seal containing Tutankhamun's cartouche on the lower section of the plaster over the doorway. Towards the bottom of the stairway he also found an assortment of broken pots and boxes, some bearing the names of Akhenaten and Smenkhare as well as that of Tutankhamun, leading him to conclude that the tomb had been used as a cache for the mummies of the pharaohs of the Amarna Period. This, Carter initially thought, would explain why the tomb had been opened and resealed on a number of occasions, although this theory would later prove to be incorrect.

The stonework and plaster blocking in the doorway was photographed and quickly removed, exposing the rubble-filled corridor. Over the next two days this was cleared out to reveal a second blocked and sealed doorway. On 26

November, Carter made a small hole in this second doorway and held a candle up to the hole so he could see through. In his book, *The Tomb of Tut.ankh.Amen*, Carter would later recall the moment:

> At first I could see nothing, the hot air escaping from the chamber causing the candle flame to flicker, but presently, as my eyes grew accustomed to the light, details of the room within emerged slowly from the mist, strange animals, statues and gold - everywhere the glint of gold. For the moment – an eternity it must have seemed to the others standing by – I was struck dumb with amazement, and when Lord Carnarvon, unable to stand the suspense any longer, inquired anxiously, 'Can you see anything?' it was all I could do to get the words out, 'Yes, wonderful things'.

The official tomb opening was scheduled for 29 November but it is hardly surprising that Carter, along with Carnarvon, Lady Evelyn and the architect Arthur Challender, an old friend of Carter's, entered the tomb themselves before this date. Challender rigged up electric lighting, illuminating the jumble of grave goods, including gilded couches, chests, thrones, and shrines. They also found two more sealed door-ways, one into the annex, a storeroom stacked full with a further assortment of objects, and one into the burial chamber itself. On either side of the blocked doorway into the burial chamber stood life-size statues of Tutankhamun, each standing in a typical pose of a pharaoh, with one foot forward and with a mace and staff in its hands, guarding the entrance.

A small hole was found in this doorway and, at some stage between the discovery and the official opening, Carter, Carnarvon and Lady Evelyn squeezed through it into the burial chamber. This did not come to light until many years later and would lead to questions being asked about Carter's integrity, and to unsubstantiated accusations that Carter and the others had illicitly removed objects from the burial chamber and the adjoining treasury. Photographs of the doorway before it was opened up show a clumsy attempt to hide the hole in the bottom corner by covering it with a basket and scattering reeds around it. Had Carter been open about this episode from the start, perhaps explaining that his curiosity got the better of him or that he wanted to make sure it really was the undisturbed tomb of Tutankhamun before inviting people to witness the opening, rather than keeping it secret, these rumours would almost certainly not have begun.

Whatever the rights and wrongs of Carter's actions, the tomb was officially opened on 29 November and the news relayed to the world. It would be another three months before the press were invited into the tomb itself, after it had been cleared sufficiently to allow enough room for this to happen, but the news of such an extraordinary discovery made headlines around the world from the moment it became known. Although robbers had entered the tomb on a number of occasions and had removed a number of items, it appeared as though they had been prevented from disturbing the burial itself and the majority of the grave goods were intact. It was the first, and remains the only, time a tomb of an Egyptian pharaoh has been found in such a well-preserved condition and it made Howard Carter a household name around the world.

Tragedy and Revelation

After the euphoria of the discovery Carter was quick to realise the huge amount of work needed to clear the tomb to the standard of archaeological excellence to which he aspired – one that, in the light of how most excavations were conducted at the time, was very high. Carnarvon appears to have been a little slower to catch on, initially saying he thought Carter had some weeks of hard work ahead of him. No doubt Carter quickly disillusioned his sponsor of any expectations he may have had about a quick resolution to the work and about when the point would arrive at which Carnarvon could expect to collect his share of the spoils.

Amongst the first things Carter did was to contact a number of other archaeologists to ask them to help with the clearance of the tomb and, within a few weeks, a team of American and British archaeologists came together. They included Arthur Mace, who had many years of experience in Egypt, the chemist Alfred Lucas, who would analyse and conserve the materials in the tomb, and Percy Newberry, the man who gave Carter his start in Egypt 30 years before. Harry Burton was given the job of photographing the whole process, setting up a dark room in a nearby tomb for the purpose, and Arthur Challender was to put his knowledge of architecture and engineering to good use when it came to removing the gilded shrines from around Tutankhamun's sarcophagus and then rigging up a pulley system to remove the lid of the sarcophagus and the coffins from inside it. One of the less well-known members of the team was Acting Sergeant Richard Adamson, who looked after the security of the tomb for seven out of the ten seasons it took to finish the job. He would later say he spent many nights in the antechamber, entertaining himself by listening to opera records on a gramophone, the noise of which, he thought, would be enough to put off most potential robbers.

As the methodical work to clear the tomb continued, it was constantly interrupted by a stream of visitors. The press were also clamouring for stories, attempting to fill the apparently insatiable appetite for news about the find from around the world. Whenever an object was brought out of the tomb, Carter and his team had to push their way through the reporters, attempting to prevent any of the finds from getting damaged as they did so. Carnarvon's decision to sell the exclusive newspaper rights to *The Times* initially appeared to be a solution to this problem – and it generated some extra finance for the excavation – but it also succeeded in turning the rest of the press against the whole enterprise. It did not go down well in Egypt either, being taken as an insult against the country and another example of the arrogant colonial attitudes of the British in general.

Towards the end of February 1923, tension was developing within the excavation team, leading to a serious argument between Carter and Carnarvon. Gossip mongers attributed this to Carnarvon's disapproval of a relationship supposedly developing between Carter, who was 48 at the time, and Lady Evelyn, Carnarvon's 22-year-old daughter. Whether or not there was any truth in the rumours, it appears more likely the argument started over a difference of opinion in how to deal with the Egyptian Government, which was considering claiming the entire contents of the tomb for the Egyptian people. Under the terms of the concession, if the tomb was considered to be intact when it was found, the Egyptians had the right to everything. Carter thought that the best course of action was to agree to hand over all the finds to the government but Carnarvon, who had invested a considerable amount of money in the expectation of getting a return, did not agree.

Whatever the cause of the disagreement, it became so serious that Carter ordered Carnarvon out of his house and closed down the excavation. Carnarvon appeared to blame himself for the rift and sent Carter a note saying:

> I have done many foolish things and I am very sorry. But there is only one thing I want to say to you which I hope you will always remember – whatever your feelings are or will be for me in the future my affection for you will never change.

Within days of sending the note, Carnarvon had become seriously ill. While shaving in his room in the Winter Palace Hotel he is said to have cut through a mosquito bite on his cheek which subsequently became infected. Carnarvon had not been a well man since the car crash in 1901 and the added stress of the excavation, together with the tension between himself and Carter, cannot have helped his condition. The infection developed into blood poisoning and then pneumonia set in. Carnarvon died in the early hours of 5 April 1923 at the age of 57.

The press were not about to let go of the antagonism they had developed towards Carnarvon over the preferential treatment he had given to *The Times*. Sensational stories about the tomb being cursed were circulated and one journalist even invented a text for the curse ('Death shall come on swift wings to him who disturbs the peace of the king') which he claimed to have found in the tomb. Journalists also reported the lights going out in Cairo at the time of Carnarvon's death and, ignoring the fact that power cuts were a common enough experience in the city at the time, claimed that this was a sign of the curse. Carnarvon's dog was also said to have died in Highclere Castle at exactly the same moment as its master.

Carter was not having any of it and, with the support of Carnarvon's widow, returned to work in the tomb. By the following February, work on the clearance had progressed to the extent that Carter was ready to remove the lid from Tutankhamun's sarcophagus. Challender rigged up a system of ropes and pulleys to lift the ton and a half weight of the lid and, on 12 February, it was raised off the body of the sarcophagus in front of an invited group of archaeologists and Egyptian officials. At first all that could be seen were linen shrouds but, when Carter pushed these back, he revealed the first of what would turn out to be three anthropoid coffins carved into the likeness of Tutankhamun.

The following day Carter had planned to give the wives and families of the people who had worked in the tomb a guided tour but he was prevented from doing so by the Egyptian Ministry of Works. He was outraged at what he considered a blatant attempt by the Egyptian Government to take over the running of the excavation and immediately stopped work, putting up a notice in the lobby of the Winter Palace Hotel to explain his actions:

Owing to the impossible restrictions and discourtesies on the part of the Public Works Department and its Antiquities Service, all my collaborators, as a protest, have refused to work any further upon their scientific investigations of the tomb of Tut.ankh.Amen. I am therefore obliged to make known to the public that, immediately after the press view of the tomb this morning, between 10am and noon, the tomb will be closed and no further work will be carried out.

It was exactly what the government had wanted him to do. For all his qualities, Carter was no diplomat or politician and, without Carnarvon to deal with the authorities, he had fallen straight into their trap. The government cancelled the concession, saying Carter had breached its terms. Matters were not helped when a wooden head depicting Tutankhamun was found packed in a crate. It looked as if Carter was trying to remove it from the site without going through official channels.

It took a year to sort out the impasse. The Egyptian Government eventually realised Carter was by far the best man to finish the work he had begun in the tomb and offered to share the concession with him. Lady Carnarvon gave up any claim she had on the contents of the tomb and received £36,000 in compensation from the Egyptian Government for the expenses Lord Carnarvon had incurred in financing the whole project.

Work began again in 1925 and, in the following year, the coffins were opened, revealing the golden funeral mask and the mummy of Tutankhamun. It was the culmination of Carter's career but by no means the end of the work in the tomb which would continue under his direction until 1932. By that time, the entire contents of the tomb, with the exception of the sarcophagus, had been transferred to the Egyptian

Museum in Cairo, where everything remains today, except for Tutankhamun's mummy, which was returned to its resting place in the tomb.

After he finished work in the tomb, Carter returned to England, where he would spend the remaining seven years of his life writing about Tutankhamun and giving lectures. Although he published a popular account of the discovery, the work of producing a full report on the whole project proved to be too much for him. In his later years he appeared to have grown tired of the enterprise. He died on 2 March 1932 and, during his lifetime, received no official recognition from either the British or Egyptian Governments to acknowledge his achievements.

Tutankhamun and the Modern World

Egyptomania

The discovery of Tutankhamun's tomb propelled the previously obscure and largely forgotten pharaoh into the glare of the modern media world, giving him celebrity status among the general public. The level of interest was unprecedented for any archaeological find and had some enduring effects on the perception of Egyptology and archaeology as a whole. Before the discovery, Egyptology had been the preserve of the idle rich and the small number of specialist archaeologists they employed but, with such intense public interest and many more people wanting to become involved, the field now began to open up into the broad academic subject it is today. The pioneering work of such figures as Sir Flinders Petrie had advanced the study of Egypt, bringing it more into line with mainstream archaeology, but it was the finds in Tutankhamun's tomb which brought it fully to the attention of the academic world. Howard Carter's work was the first time a tomb had been cleared with an eye to what could be learned from the site as a whole, rather than the objects of interest it contained being removed as quickly as possible.

The public perception of Ancient Egypt was, if anything, changed to an even greater extent than the academic one.

Millions of people suddenly became aware of archaeology and an ancient civilisation to a much higher level of knowledge than had been the case at any stage in the past. In addition to the extraordinary objects recovered, this has, perhaps, been the most enduring legacy of the discovery of the tomb. A wide section of society, which had once, through fabulous stories of mummies and curses, seen Egypt as strange and exotic, was now introduced to real archaeology. Many people became fascinated with Egypt and the pharaohs through Howard Carter's own account of his work together with multitudes of other books and articles on Egyptology and various other archaeological subjects.

A fascination with all things Egyptian did not, of course, start with Tutankhamun. Egyptomania, as it is sometimes called, had appeared in Western culture many years before the discovery of the tomb. Pharaohs, mummies, the pyramids and many other Egyptian motifs had spread through the culture of the West, exerting an influence on literature, music, art and architecture, and taking on meanings far removed from any they may originally have had. The imagery of Egypt was exploited to explore contemporary concerns and preoccupations and also for its entertainment value alone.

Examples of such Egyptian motifs in Western art forms are far too numerous to attempt to list here, so the following is a small sample to illustrate the whole. Shelley used the voice of a pharaoh in his poem 'Ozymandias', first published in 1818, to articulate the ephemeral nature of life by describing a few desolate ruins as all that remained of a great king's works. Verdi's 1871 opera *Aida* concerned the tragic fate of an Ethiopian princess taken prisoner by a pharaoh. More popular representations of Egypt appeared in British penny dreadfuls and American dime novels of the nineteenth century, under titles like *The Curse of the Mummy's Tomb*, and in the slightly more upmarket novels by Edgar Allan Poe and Louisa May Alcott. These stories can themselves be seen as the forerunners of such Hollywood films as *The Mummy* from 1999, although this has, perhaps, more to do with Indiana Jones and zombie films than it does with Ancient Egypt.

Tutankhamun's contribution to the popular canon of story-telling comes in the shape of the media-generated story of the curse of the tomb, in which an archaeological excavation is given a twist to make it more mysterious and unknown. The curse was something of an antidote to the seriousness of the academic approach to the subject, perhaps even an attempt to puncture some of the patronising superiority occasionally exhibited by highly educated archaeologists. The veracity of the story, which was quite obviously a device employed to sell more newspapers, is hardly the point. The idea of the people who disturbed the tomb of Tutankhamun being subjected to a 3,000-year-old curse is a good story and it excited the imagination of the general public, which is probably the main reason why the story has been retold again and again.

The death of Lord Carnarvon may have provided the starting point for the story but, from then on, any bad luck or misfortune occurring to anybody involved with Tutankhamun was considered by some to be a result of the effects of the curse. Howard Carter's pet canary, for example, is said to have been eaten by a snake at the exact moment as the first step leading down to the tomb was found. More recently, Dr Zahi Hawass has reported, with his tongue firmly in his cheek, that the curse struck during the project to take a CT scan of Tutankhamun's remains. He was almost involved in an accident on the drive to the Valley of the Kings and, once he was actually there, the highly expensive and sophisticated scanner didn't work. The project team began to discuss the curse, until the scanner was found to have overheated in the confined tomb and electric fans were brought in to cool it down again.

In what can be seen as an academic riposte to these stories, statistical studies have been carried out, presumably by people who didn't have anything better to do, on the life expectancies of the people involved in the discovery and clearance of the tomb when compared to those in the general population. Not surprisingly, no significant differences were found, although anybody who was actually likely to be convinced by statistics would probably not have needed convincing in the first place. A piece of anecdotal evidence gives a much clearer refutation to the story of the curse. Lord Carnarvon may have died within months of the discovery, but his daughter, Lady Evelyn Herbert, who was with him the first time he entered the tomb, lived for a further 57 years after the event, dying at the age of 79.

Exhibitions

If the discovery of the tomb introduced Tutankhamun to the modern world, high-profile touring exhibitions have returned him to the attention of successive generations. In 1972, a selection of 50 of the most precious objects from the Egyptian Museum in Cairo toured the world in the Treasures of Tutankhamun Exhibition. Millions of people in Britain, America and numerous other countries around the world were given the opportunity to see some of these extraordinary finds. In Britain alone, 1.7 million people saw the treasures, still a record number of visitors for any exhibition at the British Museum. The solid gold funeral mask was included and, together with the pyramids of Giza, this has become one the most famous and iconic images of Egypt, a symbol of the fantastic wealth and power of the pharaohs. It is considered by many to be the most beautiful object remaining from the ancient world.

Thirty-five years later another exhibition, Tutankhamun and the Golden Age of the Pharaohs, has toured America, stopping in Los Angeles, Fort Lauderdale, Chicago and Philadelphia, before arriving in London in November 2007. Some of the most famous artefacts, including the funeral mask, have not been part of this exhibition, because the Egyptian Government decided not to allow them to leave the country. Although the absence of these objects has caused a certain amount of disappointment, it has also given the curators of the exhibition the opportunity to include exhibits never before seen outside Egypt. About half the artefacts are from Tutankhamun's tomb, with the remainder being made up of objects relating to the other pharaohs of the 18th Dynasty and their families, including Amenhotep III, Akhenaten, Nefertiti and Kiya. A selection of everyday objects found in Tutankhamun's tomb has also been included, which may not be the most spectacular of the exhibits on display, but can tell us more about Egyptian society of the period than the highly decorative regal and ritual items.

The inclusion of these objects is, perhaps, a reflection of the changing emphasis of Egyptology and archaeology as a whole. From being concerned primarily with making collections of objects and an appreciation of them in terms of their artistic value, archaeology has become more interested in the analysis and interpretation of data from excavations. Attention has shifted from studying royal and political elites alone to a consideration of the societies of which these elites were part. The recent exhibition is about Tutankhamun and the pharaohs of the 18th Dynasty but, by allowing Tutankhamun to be understood within the context of the period in which he lived, it can also be seen as in line with these general trends in archaeology.

Tutankhamun in Egypt Today

Wonderful as the touring exhibitions have been, the best place to go to appreciate Tutankhamun can only be Egypt itself. Despite a number of acts of terrorism aimed specifically at tourists, Egypt is still a popular destination for visitors, not only because of the climate, but also because of its extraordinary history. For anybody interested in archaeology, it remains one of the best places in the world to visit, with spectacular sites all the way along the course of the Nile, from Alexandria in the north to Aswan in the south. There are, of course, two specific places to visit which relate to Tutankhamun: his tomb in the Valley of the Kings and the Egyptian Museum in Cairo.

The tomb is open to the public and, although visitor numbers have been restricted by the Supreme Council of Antiquities to protect it from damage, it remains one of the most visited sites in Upper Egypt. The remains of Tutankhamun's mummy, after it had been unwrapped by Howard Carter and his team, were returned to the sarcophagus in the tomb, where they rest in the outermost of his three coffins. Apart from the sarcophagus, the tomb is empty, with almost everything else being held in the Egyptian Museum in Cairo. Two galleries are dedicated to Tutankhamun, exhibiting 1,700 of the more than 5,000 items recovered from the tomb. All of the most famous artefacts, including Tutankhamun's funeral mask, his solid gold inner coffin and the gilded shrines which surrounded the sarcophagus are on permanent display.

The Egyptian museum contains by far the best collection of Egyptian artefacts of any museum in the world but this venerable old institution has been showing signs of its age for many years. The arrangement of exhibits has always been somewhat random, as have the presence and accuracy of the labelling. While this air of slight disorder can add to the charms of the museum, actually seeing the exhibits can be a frustrating experience. The sheer number of objects on display is certainly impressive, and can be overwhelming, but they represent a fraction of the number of artefacts held by the museum in total. The basement is famously supposed to contain treasures which would put any other museum's Egyptian collection to shame, but which have hardly ever been displayed because of the competition for space in the public areas of the museum.

The Egyptian Government is in the process of remedying this situation. A new museum, to be known as the Grand Egyptian Museum, is being built on the Giza Plateau, not far from the pyramids and well away from the noise and pollution of central Cairo. It is scheduled to open in 2010 and will include what is described on the official website as 'a museum within a museum' of the artefacts from Tutankhamun's tomb.

Some of the press releases from the Egyptian Government have given the impression that the new museum will be more like a theme park than a cultural institution where people can enjoy the Tutankhamun experience. Hopefully, the curators of the new museum can achieve the balancing act of making the exhibitions accessible without insulting the intelligence of the general public.

Recent Finds

In February 2006, Dr Zahi Hawass announced to the world's press the discovery of a new tomb in the Valley of the Kings, designated as KV63, by a team of archaeologists from the University of Memphis (Tennessee) led by Dr Otto Schaden. It was considered to be the most important find in the valley since Howard Carter uncovered Tutankhamun's tomb in 1922 and sparked a media frenzy. The fact that it was found close to Tutankhamun's tomb prompted a great deal of speculation about the possible identity of the owner of the tomb.

The doorway to the tomb was unsealed and looked as if it had been opened a number of times in antiquity. When the tomb was opened in the 2006 digging season, Schaden found a single chamber with undecorated walls, which resembled some of the tombs built in the 18th Dynasty for the nobility, such as that of Yuya and Tuyu (KV46), rather than those built for the pharaohs. It contained seven coffins, five large ones and two for children, all of which were stacked together towards the back of the chamber, and 28 large storage jars. All of the coffins were anthropoid and had been painted, although much of the decoration was covered in layers of black resin and the wood was damaged by termites. Only two of them were sealed, one of the large ones and one of the child-sized ones, meaning only these two could potentially contain mummies. Unfortunately, when they were opened, neither one did. The smaller coffin was stuffed with what appeared to be pillows, an extremely rare find from the ancient world, and, underneath the pillows, there was a pink gold coffinette. The other was filled with various materials used in the embalming process, including bags of natron. The storage jars also contained materials associated with embalming and other artefacts associated with 18th Dynasty royal funerals.

The large, sealed coffin may not have contained a mummy when it was opened, but the impression of a body remained in the bottom, showing that it had been used at some stage. The coffin lid had been carved with the image of a female figure with its arms crossed, the typical pose for a member of the royal family, and hieroglyphic inscriptions could be made out underneath a covering of black resin. At the time of writing (Summer 2007) a transliteration of these inscriptions has not been made public but it is possible they will identify its original occupant. From the artwork on the front of the coffin, Dr Zahi Hawass made a tentative identification of it as the one belonging to Kiya, one of Akhenaten's wives who is often said to be Tutankhamun's mother. The proximity of the chamber to Tutankhamun's tomb was given as another reason for this identification, although, since it does not appear to have actually been a tomb, this does not necessarily follow. The artefacts found in the chamber suggest it was used as a cache of funeral equipment for another burial, in the same way as the chamber found by Theodore Davis in 1909 (KV54) had been for Tutankhamun.

After the discovery of the new chamber, it emerged that a

team of archaeologists from the Amarna Royal Tombs Project, led by Nicholas Reeves, had investigated the area where KV63 was found with ground-penetrating radar a few years previously. The radar survey had shown an anomaly in the rock in the position where the chamber would later be found and had been interpreted at the time as showing the presence of a tomb or chamber of some sort. Much to the annoyance of Dr Hawass and the Supreme Council of Antiquities (SCA), Reeves also announced a further radar anomaly not far from KV63 which he said could be another undiscovered tomb. He designated this KV64 but, because nothing has physically been found, this designation has not been officially recognised by the SCA. According to the regulations set out by the SCA, tomb designations can only be made through them, as the Egyptian Government body responsible for the Valley of the Kings, so the presence or otherwise of an undiscovered tomb has become something of a controversial subject. This has not stopped speculation about the possibility of this tomb being found at some point in the future and on what it could contain. Reeves has proposed that it could be the tomb of a member of the royal family from the Amarna Period, even, perhaps, the tomb of Nefertiti, one of the Holy Grails of Egyptology, but there is no way of verifying these claims until the actual tomb, if there really is one, is found and opened.

New discoveries are, of course, always exciting but there are plenty of other areas where further research could reveal more details about Tutankhamun and the 18th Dynasty in general. The Egyptian Mummy Project is an ongoing attempt to study all of the mummies known to exist in Egypt using CT scans and other technology to resolve such questions as the family relationships between the pharaohs. Although DNA analysis is not always accurate when dealing with 3,000-year-old mummies, and a high potential for contamination with foreign DNA is one of the main problems, it is now being used regularly and has the potential to provide all sorts of new insights into the 18th Dynasty royal families. There are apparently no current plans to use DNA analysis on Tutankhamun's remains but, at some stage in the future, it must surely happen. The results of any such testing would not suddenly fill in all the blanks in our knowledge of Tutankhamun's life but they might lead to a better understanding of who he was.

In the final analysis, the combination of new archaeological discoveries and the use of increasing technology to investigate and interpret both them and the discoveries made in the past can only enhance our knowledge and appreciation of Tutankhamun and the world in which he lived.

Appendix 1

A Chronology of Ancient Egypt

Pre-dynastic Period (the Neolithic, including the Naqata Period)	5000–3000 BC
Early Dynastic Period (1st and 2nd Dynasties)	3000–2686 BC
Old Kingdom (3rd to 8th Dynasties)	2686–2160 BC
First Intermediate Period (9th and 10th Dynasties)	2160–2055 BC
Middle Kingdom (11th to 14th Dynasties)	2055–1650 BC
Second Intermediate Period (15th to 17th Dynasties, including the Hyksos)	1650–1550 BC
New Kingdom (18th to 20th Dynasties)	1550–1069 BC
Third Intermediate Period (21st to 25th Dynasties)	1069–664 BC

Late Period
(26th Dynasty to Persian Period)   664–332 BC

Ptolemaic Period
(Macedonian and Ptolemaic Dynasties)   332–30 BC

Roman Period   30 BC–AD 395

Appendix 2

Pharaohs of the 18th Dynasty

Ahmose	1550–1525 BC
Amenhotep I	1525–1504 BC
Thutmose I	1504–1492 BC
Thutmose II	1492–1479 BC
Thutmose III	1479–1425 BC
Hatshepsut	1473–1458 BC
Amenhotep II	1427–1400 BC
Thutmose IV	1400–1390 BC
Amenhotep III	1352–1336 BC
Akhenaten	1352–1336 BC
Smenkhare/Neferneferuaten	1338–1336 BC
Tutankhamun	1336–1327 BC
Ay	1327–1323 BC
Horemheb	1323–1295 BC

Glossary

akh The form taken by the blessed dead after they had successfully negotiated the journey into the underworld.

Amun A local god of Thebes who rose in prominence during the 18th Dynasty to become one of the most important of the gods.

Anubis The jackal-headed god of the dead, particularly associated with embalming and mummification.

The Aten Representation of the sun disc, worshipped to the exclusion of all the other gods during the Amarna Period.

ba The non-physical aspects of the body, sometimes equated with the modern idea of the personality.

canopic jar A container used to hold the embalmed viscera and internal organs removed from a body during mummification and placed in the tomb.

cartouche The elliptical outline around the names of pharaohs to protect the name from evil.

Hittites A people and an empire centred on Anatolia, contemporary with the 18th Dynasty, who were continually in conflict with Egypt in Syria.

Horus The falcon-headed god, associated with the sun disc and the pharaoh.

Hyksos Migrants into the Nile Delta, beginning in the Middle Kingdom, who rose to power in Lower Egypt in the Second Intermediate Period.

Isis Goddess who was the wife of Osiris and mother of Horus and associated with the ideal qualities of a woman.

ka The quality of a living person that differentiated him or her from the dead; can be equated with the spirit.

Maat Goddess personifying truth, justice and the essential harmony of the universe.

Mitanni People of the Hurrian Empire in northern Syria, sometime opponents and allies of Egypt.

natron A naturally occurring mineral salt, mostly sodium carbonate and sodium bicarbonate, used in the mummification process.

nemes headdress The stripped head cloth worn by a pharaoh.

Osiris God of the underworld associated with resurrection and fertility.

Ra The sun god, one of the most influential of all the Egyptian gods, who was often worshipped in association with another god, including Amun, as Amun-Ra, and Horus, as Ra-Horakhty.

shabti A funerary figurine, placed in the tomb to do the manual labour required by the dead person in the afterlife.

stele Slab of stone or wood bearing an inscription.

vizier Modern term for the holders of the Egyptian title Tjaty, a chief minister of either Upper or Lower Egypt.

Further Resources

Books

Aldred, Cyril, *Akhenaten: King of Egypt*, London: Thames and Hudson, 1991

Carter, Howard and Mace, AC, *The Tomb of Tutankhamun*, Washington, DC: National Geographic, new ed., 2003

Dodson, Aidan, *The Complete Royal Families of Ancient Egypt*, London: Thames and Hudson, 2004

Haag, Michael, *The Rough Guide to Tutankhamun*, London: Rough Guides, 2005

Hawass, Zahi, *Tutankhamun and the Golden Age of the Pharaohs*, Washington, DC: National Geographic, 2005

Hornurg, Erik, *Akhenaten and the Religion of Light*, Ithaca, NY: Cornell University Press, 2001

Manley, Bill, *The Penguin Historical Atlas of Ancient Egypt*, London: Penguin, 1996

Meskell, Lynn, *Private Life in New Kingdom Egypt*, Princeton, NJ: Princeton University Press, 2002

Reeves, Nicholas, *The Complete Tutankhamun: The King, the Tomb, the Royal Treasures,* London: Thames and Hudson, new ed., 2007

Reeves, Nicholas and Williamson, Richard, *The Complete Valley of the Kings*, London: Thames and Hudson, 1996

Shaw, Ian, *Ancient Egypt: A Very Short Introduction*, Oxford: Oxford University Press, 2004

Shaw, Ian (ed.), *The Oxford History of Ancient Egypt*, Oxford: Oxford University Press, 2000

Shaw, Ian and Nicholson, Paul, *The British Museum Dictionary of Ancient Egypt*, London: British Museum 2002

Tyldesley, Joyce, *Egypt: How a Lost Civilisation was Rediscovered*, London: BBC Books, 2006

Hatchepsut: The Female Pharaoh, London: Penguin, 1998

Nefertiti: Egypt's Sun Queen, London: Penguin, 2005

Williamson, Richard, *The Complete Gods and Goddesses of Ancient Egypt*, London: Thames and Hudson, 2003

Websites

www.ashmolean.org/Griffith.html
Griffith Institute in Oxford, where Howard Carter's excavation notes and diaries are held.

www.nationalgeographic.com/explorer/tut/
Official site of the Tutankhamun and the Golden Age of the Pharaohs exhibition.

www.ees.ac.uk
The Egyptian Exploration Society.

www.digitalegypt.ucl.ac.uk
Teaching resource from UCL and the Petrie Museum.

www.gem.gov.eg
Official site of the Grand Egyptian Museum project in Cairo.

www.newton.com.ac.uk/egypt
Great resource for all things to do with Egyptology.

www.guardian.net/hawass/
Official site of Dr Zahi Hawass.

www.ancientneareast.net/egypt
Details of current excavations.

www.arce.org
The American Research Center in Egypt.

http://egyptology.blogspot.com
Egyptology News, one of the best of the blogs, compiled by
Andie Byrnes.

Index